# Prisoner of War Camps in Britain During the Second World War

## By
## Jon and Diane Sutherland

**WAR IN BRITAIN SERIES**

GGP

First published in the UK in 2012 by Golden Guides Press Ltd.

10 8 6 4 2 1 3 5 7 9

ISBN (paperback) 978-1-78095-013-6
ISBN (Kindle) 978-1-78095-035-8
ISBN (ePub) 978-1-78095-036-5

Typeset in 11pt Palatino by Mac Style, Driffield, East Yorkshire.
Cover design by Mousemat Design Ltd.
Edited by Melanie Marshall.
Printed and bound in Great Britain by
Marston Book Services Limited, Didcot
EBooks produced by ePubDirect.com.

Golden Guides Press Ltd
P.O. Box 171
Newhaven
E. Sussex
BN9 1AZ
UK
admin@goldenguidespress.com
www.goldenguidespress.com

# PRISONER OF WAR CAMPS
# IN BRITAIN
## During the Second World War

WAR IN BRITAIN SERIES

## Jon & Diane Sutherland

# Contents

Introduction     6

**Chapter One**     Prisoner of War Camps     12

**Chapter Two**     Locations in England     28

**Chapter Three**     Locations in the Rest of the British Isles     124

**Chapter Four**     Escapes     159

**Chapter Five**     The Bonzos     175

**Chapter Six**     Staying On or Going Home     183

**Chapter Seven**     The Legacy of the Camps and Prisoners     196

Bibliography     209

Index     211

# Introduction

IN THE period roughly falling between 1942 and 1948, the British Isles received an influx of around half a million enemy prisoners of war. It was an influx of migrants that had been caused as a result of the growing success of the Allied cause over the course of the Second World War. This led to a construction of a vast network of purpose-built camps, hastily requisitioned existing buildings, tented communities and hostels across the length and breadth of Britain.

To date, these prisoner of war camps and the lasting impact that this massive migration had on the British Isles has been largely ignored. Unfortunately, there are very few official records about the prisoner of war camps. What does seem to remain is references to the post-war period only. Some local communities have tried to preserve what is left of these camps, but the impact of their efforts has not been wholly successful.

At the peak there were nearly 400 major prisoner of war camps in England, Scotland, Northern Ireland and Wales. Unfortunately many of the prisoner of war camps were temporary affairs. Most of the buildings were made of timber or of corrugated iron, and these were demolished, their parts being sold off and the sites redeveloped for industry or for housing. In fact even to this day there is no central register of the site of every camp and there is even confusion about the precise location of many of the camps, particularly the hostels. This is in stark contrast to prisoner of war camps in Germany, the most notable of which is Colditz, which is still wholly intact and is of enormous historical significance.

The main influx of enemy prisoners of war took place after the successes in North Africa, in late 1942. Initially the prisoners of war were largely Italian, but after Operation Overlord, the landings in Normandy, which culminated in the liberation of France and other western countries, it was German prisoners of war that began to flood into Britain.

The influx of prisoners of war before 1944 had been well managed. Initially they were brought into the camp system and then dispersed around the country in order to carry out manual or farm labour. The whole camp system came under huge pressure between 1944 and 1948. Huge numbers of German prisoners of war were brought to Britain. As a prime example, in March 1941 Britain held just 550 German prisoners of war. At its peak in September 1946, that figure was 402,200. There had been a steady increase of 40 to 50,000 from September 1944. By December 1946 the peak had fallen away and Germans were being repatriated at

Prisoners captured in fighting in the El Alamein area [*Image courtesy of Library of Congress Prints and Photographs division 3c32809u.*]

a rate of between 40 and 60,000 per month. This meant that by June 1948 there were just 2,790 Germans left in prisoner of war camps in Britain.

Obviously, the first Germans to arrive as prisoners of war were those that belonged to the German merchant navy, the Kriegsmarine, submarine crews and members of the Luftwaffe. They were in relatively small numbers and could be interrogated and screened before being allocated to a prisoner of war camp. The Germans were graded according to their political views and often by the branch of the armed forces in which they had served. Hence ardent Nazis and members of the SS were graded as hardcore Nazis, or 'black' prisoners of war. These men presented a problem and they had to be held under the strictest of military conditions. Most of the other men, the 'whites' and the 'greys' were still subject to camp discipline, but were given significantly more freedom and they were also allowed to work.

Throughout the course of the Second World War some 3.5 million Germans became prisoners of war of the British alone. Hence the 402,000 maximum represents little more than 15 per cent of the total German prisoner community. Many were shipped to Canada, others were temporarily held in the United States but vast numbers never made it out of the country in which they had been captured, notably France or Holland.

Along with the prisoners of war essentially being used as forced manual labourers came significant moral arguments. It was hotly debated in the House of Lords and the House of Commons and there were many that believed that at the earliest possible juncture the Italians and Germans should be returned home. However there was another reason for hanging on to them and that was the acute labour shortage.

In fact German prisoners of war were not used for labour until around August 1944. This had not been the case with the Italians and whole areas of the British Isles in terms of agriculture would have collapsed without the thousands of Italians working on farms up and down the country. This brought about the creation of the work camp, but the problem was that prisoners needed to travel large distances from the camp to where they were required to work. This brought about a change in the system and saw the establishment of hostels.

Initially each of the working camps would have around three hostels. Each of the hostels would have some 50 to 70 prisoners of war. The idea was that the prisoners could operate in a three-mile diameter from the hostel. The situation, however, changed once again in September 1943 when the Italians surrendered. The Italians were offered a stark choice; they could cooperate and enjoy a greater degree of freedom and be paid, or they could class themselves as belligerents and would remain within a prison camp system. Ultimately this would lead to the development of over 100 labour camps and 80 main camps across the whole of the British Isles.

The situation with the Germans was somewhat different. Britain needed to use prisoner of war labour. As the Italians were being repatriated, Germans took their place. It is a sign of how many Italians were still prepared to remain in Britain that in August 1945, almost two years after the Italian surrender, that there were still more than 73,000 Italians in either camps, hostels or farms. It was proposed that by the end of 1946, all of the Italians should be repatriated.

German prisoners of war being held on mainland Europe would be brought to Britain to fill the void. There were dissenting voices about these plans because having this number of prisoners of war meant a drain on Britain's resources. Nonetheless, first the Italians and then the Germans would make a massive contribution towards agriculture and industrial productivity.

By May 1946 there were 163,000 Germans working in agriculture and 116,000 engaged in other work. As can be expected, there was no clear blueprint regarding what a prisoner of war camp in Britain should look like. With a network of 1,500 by the end of 1946, some of them resembled the archetypal prisoner of war camp, consisting of a number of huts to be used as sleeping quarters, other huts or tents operating as canteens, theatres, hospitals, libraries and stores. These would all be surrounded by layers of fencing and barbed wire and attached to the camp would be barracks for the camp guards.

The most familiar type of hut was of course the Nissen hut, which was a semicircular building. It was easy to put up and could be bolted together by relatively unskilled labour. Towards the end of 1943 the British began fabricating lightweight timber framed huts, which could be erected on top of brick or concrete foundations. The idea with these is that they could be easily dismantled and erected elsewhere as needed.

Choosing the sites for the prisoner of war camps was always a difficult matter. In the early stages of the war it was obvious to make sure that the prisoner of war camps were nowhere near possible invasion areas. The second issue was not to put prisoners in secure areas, such as airfields or military headquarters. It was feared that if any of the prisoners escaped then they could provide vital intelligence to the enemy. The trouble was that the sites needed water, drainage, electricity and access. It fell on the Ministry of Works and Planning to recommend suitable sites.

It is interesting to note that there were obviously other considerations when siting the prisoner of war camps. A huge number of them were sited in areas where there was arable farming. England had over 80 per cent of all of the prisoner of war camps. Scotland had around 10 per cent and the balance of the British Isles, Wales, Northern Ireland and the Channel Islands, had the remaining 10 per cent.

Unlike the French, who had some 50,000 Germans working in coal mines in March 1945, the majority of the German prisoners of war in Britain worked on the land. There was a considerable number who were building housing and smaller numbers involved in timber production, quarrying, maintaining canals, iron and steel work and coal distribution. Some of the men in their previous civilian lives had skills that Britain badly needed in the immediate post-war years. The Germans were paid an hourly rate, which could net them 6s for a 48-hour week. In comparison, a labourer in Britain had a minimum wage of 75s a week.

Whilst so much time and effort is given to preserving pillboxes or anti-tank obstacles and other remnants of the Second World War in the British Isles, so little money or interest has been lavished on the prisoner of war camps. Some of the camps have been lucky in as much as they have enjoyed a second existence as an army camp or an industrial estate. Yet as we will see as we examine the spread of the prisoner of war camps across the country, you can find them under post-war housing estates, in the grounds of grand country houses or perhaps under the car park of an out-of-town retail park.

It is vital that what remains of these camps is recorded before they finally disappear. A handful of the sites in decent states of preservation seem to have their future assured. But most are gone and the vast majority that do remain are in a precarious and fragile state, which without attention will see them disappear forever.

After reading this book you may be amazed to discover that you are actually walking on the site of a former prisoner of war camp, or that an odd building on the outskirts of your town or village was not an army depot, but was in fact home to hundreds if not thousands of Italians and Germans in the 1940s.

# Chapter One

# Prisoner of War Camps

B Y THE time Victory in Europe was declared on 7th May, 1945 there was already an incredible 400,000 or more Germans alone being held prisoner in an estimated 1,500 camps in Great Britain. This was in addition to the huge numbers of Italian prisoners of war, some of which had been behind barbed wire for nearly five years.

Huge numbers of German and Italian prisoners of war had already been sent to Canada or the United States of America. Vast numbers of Germans had been scooped up in the last phases of the war on the Western Front, as Allied forces penetrated into Germany. There would still be tens of thousands working in agriculture until 1946 and beyond. Yet this state of affairs for captured enemy servicemen was by no means new.

### What was a prisoner of war?
The term prisoner of war probably dates back to the Seventeenth Century and was used to describe an enemy combatant, or in some cases a civilian, who was being held in custody by an enemy power.

In ancient times, to be captured by the enemy would either mean death or slavery. In fact it is widely believed that many of the original gladiators that fought across the Roman Empire to entertain the masses were prisoners of war. Some of the specialist names used to describe particular types of gladiator come from the names of tribes that fought and ultimately lost against the Romans, such as the Gaul, Thracian and Samnite.

It was not always the case that prisoners of war were killed or permanently enslaved. Some were only held for a limited period of time. Many of the Greek States, for example, would keep prisoners of war only for the duration of the conflict, essentially as hostages. For many, capture meant a life of slavery, unless someone could buy their freedom for them. But this would first mean knowing that they had survived.

A very early change to all of this was contained in a code of conduct attributed to Muhammad, the founder of the religion of Islam. Under reforms prisoners were assigned to an individual. This individual's responsibility was to ensure that the prisoner was well looked after and not ill-treated. At the end of any hostilities the prisoner would either be released or ransomed. Prior to that if enemies had been captured and could not afford a ransom then they were sold as slaves (assuming they had not been executed).

Other cultures and times saw an entirely different attitude toward enemy prisoners of war:

- In South America the Aztecs would routinely capture prisoners of war and use these prisoners as live sacrifices to their gods
- The Mongols would refuse to take prisoners of war if a city, tribe or nation attempted to resist them; all would be killed
- During the Crusades the Crusaders and their Moslem opponents would rarely take prisoners, unless of course an individual was from a rich, noble family where a ransom could be extorted

During the English wars against France, in a scene that was made famous in William Shakespeare's *Henry V*, large numbers of French prisoners were killed after the battle of Agincourt in 1415, when it was believed that a second force of French was about to attack the English. In any other circumstance these prisoners of war, particularly those with high social status and families with deep pockets, would have been ransomed.

In *Henry V*, Act 4, Scene 6, Henry, along with his men, is marching along with his prisoners. They hear an alarm and King Henry says "But hark! What new alarum is this same? The French have reinforc'd their scatter'd men. Then every soldier kill his prisoners; give the word through".

Perhaps the first set of rules concerning prisoners of war came into existence in the middle of the Seventeenth Century. The Thirty Years War, which had raged from 1618 to 1648 between essentially Protestant states and their Allies and Roman Catholic states and their Allies, had come to an end. The Peace of Westphalia was one of a number of peace treaties that aimed to end the war. In this treaty it was agreed that all prisoners of war that had been taken by either side should now be released without the payment of a ransom.

## French prisoners in England

The first really huge influx of enemy prisoners of war took place during the French Revolutionary Wars (1792–1802) and the Napoleonic Wars (1802–1815). This led to what is believed to be the first purpose-built prisoner of war camp in England, at Norman Cross, near Peterborough in Cambridgeshire. It was probably originally designed for around 4,000 prisoners. These were Frenchmen that had been captured in the West Indies. The site was chosen because it had a good water supply and it was believed that local resources could provide sufficient food. Basically it was like a fort, with accommodation blocks, each to hold 500 prisoners. In fact the average population was more like 5,500. It was originally designed to be a model of humane treatment. The prisoners were fed, offered education, there was a Catholic priest, a prison hospital and prisoners were encouraged to engage in handicrafts and sell these at local markets.

Despite the relatively humane conditions, Frenchmen did try to escape. After one such attempt, one of the prisoners stabbed a civilian in 1808. He was convicted and sentenced to death by hanging and was executed in front of all the other prisoners and their guards. In a subsequent search over 700 weapons were found hidden in the prison. Most of the French were repatriated by mid-1814 and many of the buildings were dismantled.

As an interesting footnote, Channel 4's *Time Team* excavated part of the site in 2009. They found part of a wall, an accommodation block and a burial site. At the time the work on this important site, identified as the first real prisoner of war camp in the world, was hailed as incredibly important in terms of world history.

## Andersonville

Whatever the reputation of this first prisoner of war camp, undoubtedly some of the worst cases of a system that was set up to deal with prisoners in a humane manner happened during the American Civil War (1861–1865). Around 600,000 American soldiers were killed, either Union or Confederate, during the conflict. Upwards of 10 per cent of them died in prisoner of war camps. The most notorious was the Confederate camp based at Andersonville in Georgia. It was a truly horrific place and at one time held an estimated 46,000 Union prisoners of war. More than 13,000 of the men died whilst incarcerated.

In 1998, on the site of Andersonville Prison, the National Prisoner of War Museum was opened. It covers the experiences of all American prisoners of war across history. The site also has a national cemetery, with 13,714 graves of which 921 are marked as unknown.

It was more a question of appalling management rather than outright mistreatment. The majority of the men died as a result of hunger, exposure and disease.

The Union prisoner of war camps in the north, however, were not a great deal better. At Camp Douglas, near Chicago in Illinois, around 10 per cent of the Confederates held there died of the freezing cold during one winter. Another camp in New York State, Elmira Prison, saw a quarter of the over 12,000 Confederate prisoners of war die as a result of cold weather, disease and malnutrition over just a 15-month period.

## Gradual improvements

Steps were being taken during the Nineteenth Century to try and improve both the treatment and the eventual processing leading to the release of prisoners. Early steps had been taken during the Napoleonic Wars and the War of 1812, between Britain and America. However, it took until 1874, with the Brussels

Conference, to get nations to begin to agree about humane treatment of prisoners. No hard and fast agreements were signed, but some new conventions were generally accepted and it was widely agreed that all prisoners should be treated in a humane manner.

By the beginning of the Twentieth Century the great powers, which then included Great Britain, France, the United States of America, Russia, China and Persia, were all in broad agreement about having a legally binding, international agreement. The Hague Convention of 1907 set out the general laws of war and what constituted a war crime. In fact one whole chapter of the annex to the convention covered prisoners of war in detail. Additional amendments were made in 1929 at the Third Geneva Convention. For the first time prisoners of war were actually defined and the responsibilities of the powers that had captured them were made abundantly clear.

There were vast numbers of men held as prisoners of war during the First World War. Britain and France between them held at least 720,000 and the Americans a further 48,000. Many of the German prisoners continued to be held until 1920.

## The Geneva Convention

The exact definition of a prisoner of war was clearly stated in Article 4 and it included members of organised resistance movements. This would be a major bone of contention during the Second World War, where partisans, resistance fighters and even soldiers, sailors and airmen not in full uniform were summarily executed. Equally, there would also be particularly harsh treatment meted out to particular types of soldiers. Hitler, for example, decreed his so-called 'Commando Order', which he issued on 18th October, 1942, stating that any Allied Commando, even if they were in uniform, should be treated as an enemy agent or saboteur and immediately executed. There were similar instances, although not officially sanctioned, if German Schutzstaffel (SS) troops fell into enemy hands.

The Hague Convention and the Geneva Convention should have made the plight of prisoners of war far clearer when the

Italian prisoners detraining at Wady Sarar, 21st December, 1940. [*Image courtesy of the Library of Congress Prints and Photographs division, 20926u.*]

Second World War broke out in 1939. In reality, however, the treatment of prisoners of war varied enormously. The Germans, the Japanese and the Soviets were all notorious for widespread atrocities against prisoners during the Second World War.

Some prisoners of war did not even make it off the battlefield. In one such notorious incident, at Le Paradis on 27th May, 1940, during the battle for France, nearly 100 men, mainly from the 2nd Battalion of the Royal Norfolk Regiment, were machine-gunned by members of the 14th Company of the SS Division, Totenkopf. After the war Hauptsturmführer Fritz Knöchlein, who had commanded the German unit, was executed in 1949, with two of the survivors of the massacre, giving evidence at his trial.

Hauptsturmführer Fritz Knöchlein was confined to the so-called London Cage in Kensington Palace Gardens in London, which was part of the British War Crimes Investigation Unit. It had space for 60 prisoners, had five interrogation rooms and was headed up by

Alexander Scotland, commander of the Prisoner of War Interrogation Section of the British Intelligence Corps.

## The Second World War

The treatment of prisoners, particularly Italians and Germans, during the Second World War by the Allies was broadly in line with the 1929 Geneva Convention. There were, of course, incidents when German prisoners in particular were summarily executed on the battlefield. These, however, were isolated incidents.

One incident that was made public was the so-called Dachau Massacre. This took place on 29th April, 1945, less than a week before the end of hostilities in Europe. Although testimony differs, somewhere between 10 and 100 Germans were executed by US soldiers of the 45th Infantry Division. To put this into perspective, the Americans had just entered Dachau concentration camp. The whole area was littered with the bodies of thousands of camp inmates.

Italian prisoners eating on ground. [*Image courtesy of the Library of Congress Prints and Photographs division, 20938u.*]

Most of the German camp guards had fled but around 300 SS guards surrendered. What actually happened has never been truly explained or agreed upon. An official US Army investigation broadly agreed that some of the Americans had fired during a supposed escape attempt. Other testimony suggests that not only did the Americans open fire, killing SS men and their guard dogs, but they also handed out guns to some of the inmates of the concentration camp to take their own revenge.

## Designating Italian prisoners

In the early stages of the Second World War the Allies' success against the Italians was significantly better than that against the Germans. Great Britain was fighting Italy primarily in North Africa. Italy suffered a series of serious reversals and vast numbers of Italian prisoners of war were taken. Undoubtedly it must have been a logistical nightmare to move the Italians from Egypt and back to Britain to be put into the prison camp system.

It has been estimated that around 154,000 Italians were held in Britain during the period 1941 to 1946. By September 1943 British authorities faced a serious problem. Italy surrendered in the September and effectively changed sides. The Italian prisoners of war were offered a clear choice; they could either become cooperators or non-cooperators.

Cooperators would be paid more for any work that they carried out and would be under a far less secure regime. Non-cooperators would effectively continue to operate as prisoners of war and be held under relatively secure conditions. By 1946 the majority of the Italians had been repatriated. But a conservative estimate of around 1,400 decided to stay in Britain and continue their civilian role as rural workers.

The Italians had provided more of the workforce on the land than the Germans, until the latter stages of the Second World War. By 1944 it was far more common to see German prisoners of war working on the land than it was to see Italian prisoners.

Britain's experience with the Italians, once they had proven themselves to be of good character and disinterested in escape, allowed a slackening of security. Initially all of the Italians that

Italian prisoners on a train at Wady Sarar, 21st December, 1940. [*Image courtesy of the Library of Congress Prints and Photographs division, 20954u.*]

worked on farms were marched back to their prisoner of war camp each evening. Every single man was accounted for daily. Those that worked well and displayed good behaviour would be housed in guarded hostels near their place of work. Others would be allowed to stay on the farms. This cut down an enormous amount of manpower and costs. Essentially, the farmer would take responsibility for any prisoners of war working on his land. The Italians would also be far more productive, as they could work a full day and time would not be lost in marching them backwards and forwards to secure accommodation. It took some time for this system to be transferred over to the German prisoners of war.

### Designating German prisoners
Tens of thousands of German and Italian prisoners been taken even before Allied armies began the liberation of France and Western Europe in June 1944. Many of these had been captured in North

Africa and then subsequently in fighting in Sicily and mainland Italy. But the Allies had seriously underestimated how many they would subsequently capture in their drive towards the Rhine.

The Allies had reckoned on capturing around three million German soldiers. But in fact by June 1945:

- The Americans alone had captured 5 million
- The British had a further 2.6 million
- Another 1.4 million had been captured in Italy
- It was estimated that upwards of another 1 million were struggling west to avoid becoming prisoners of war of the Soviets

This was inevitably going to cause enormous problems. At the beginning of 1945 the Americans, for example, had just over 300,000 German prisoners of war to look after. By April this had become 2.6 million and a month later it had doubled again. It was

German prisoners await their turn to take off aboard a United States army transport plane at an advanced air base in North Africa. [*Image courtesy of the Library of Congress Prints and Photographs division, 8e00965u.*]

no longer practical to be sending such huge numbers of men to the United States, as had been the case in the past. Instead a system that had to cope with in excess of 7.6 million prisoners had to be set up.

The western Allies designated enemy prisoners of war as either surrendered enemy personnel (SEP), which was the British version, or disarmed enemy forces (DEF), the US version. Of the 7.6 million that were in British or American hands by June 1945, over 4.2 million were technically proper prisoners of war, as they had been captured before Germany surrendered. The rest of them, some 3.4 million, were not technically prisoners of war. As a consequence the Americans in particular were discharging huge numbers of these men (1.2 million) and simply sending them home.

This still remained an enormous problem. Most of the rest of the Germans were put into what was called Rheinwiesenlager (Rhine Meadow Camps). These were set up by the Americans and were spread across much of western Germany and neighbouring countries. There were 19 of them and they were designed to hold around one million German prisoners of war, although approximately two million were actually held. These were truly vast camps. They would be split into between 10 and 20 sections, or individual camps, each sub-camp designed to house between 5,000 and 10,000 men. A prime example was the one at Remagen in Holland, which had been designed to hold 100,000 men but actually held 184,000.

The Rheinwiesenlager's official name was prisoner of war 'temporary enclosures'. Conditions in some of the camps were dreadful and somewhere between 3,000 and 10,000 Germans died in these camps. For some time even the International Red Cross was prevented from visiting the camps.

One American solution was to send approximately three quarters of a million German prisoners to operate as forced labourers in France. The British, on the other hand, had responsibility for German prisoners in many different locations. There were numerous prisoner of war camps dotted around Great

Britain and others in Canada. Some of their original prisoners had been transferred to the United States and now they were responsible for prisoners of war in camps across France, Belgium, Holland and western Germany.

Repatriating all of these German prisoners was a hotly debated issue. Even by 1946 British agriculture had become heavily reliant on German prisoners' labour. It was estimated that 20 per cent of all agricultural work in Britain was being carried out by German prisoners of war. There were calls to release them. Some ardent and unrepentant Nazis were still being held, particularly at Wilton Park. This was an odd place, as it was originally the Combined Services Detailed Interrogation Centre (CSDIC). This organisation was given the job of interrogating particularly high-ranking enemy prisoners of war. Ultimately, through its doors would pass the likes of Rudolph Hess and Field Marshal von Rundstedt.

The unit itself, in Buckinghamshire, was closed towards the end of 1945, with its prisoners being transferred to other camps. But then it was taken over by the Foreign Office and used to denazify German prisoners of war. Work there continued until around 1949.

In 1947 there had again been a major argument in Britain about the fate of the German prisoners of war. The Ministry of Agriculture argued that they should be kept until at least 1948 to help with the harvest. Others argued that they should be sent home. As it was, by the end of 1947, around 250,000 had indeed been sent back to Germany. Others were retained until at least November 1948. At the same time, for a wide range of reasons, around 24,000 of the prisoners of war decided to stay on in Britain.

## The changing face of enemy prisoners of war
Some of the earliest camp inmates were members of the Luftwaffe or the Kriegsmarine. Some of these men were captured as early as 1939. Any Luftwaffe aircrew that were shot down over Britain, or just offshore, were likely to fall into British hands. Kriegsmarine U-boats were operating all around the coasts of Britain, particularly in the North Sea and in the Atlantic. The chances of survival were slim if the Royal Navy spotted them. In fact, of the

around 40,000 U-boat crewmen that operated during the whole of the Second World War, only around a quarter of them survived.

There were some notable exceptions. On 20th September, 1939 the U-27, commanded by Johannes Franz, was operating off the west of Scotland. It was spotted by the Royal Navy destroyers, HMS *Fortune,* HMS *Faulknor* and HMS *Forester.* They depth charged the U-27 and all 38 crewmen were captured and became prisoners of war.

The U-27 was in fact the second German submarine to be sunk in the Second World War. The U-39 had been sunk on 14th September off the northwest coast of Ireland and all of her crewmembers survived and were captured.

Many of the early prisoners of war were shipped out of Britain and either to Canada or the United States. These prisoners were not entirely happy about the situation, not least of which was the fact that they could be sunk by their own U-boats en route across the Atlantic.

Britain welcomed a steady stream of prisoners of war until the trickle became a flood in the middle of 1943. Crushing victories, first in North Africa and then enormous gains in France from mid-1944 saw huge numbers of German prisoners. It should be borne in mind that entire armies were being captured. In fact very few Germans or Italians escaped North Africa when hostilities ended there at Tunis in Tunisia on 13th May. Many of these prisoners, rather than being shipped to Britain were in fact transported straight across the Atlantic to North America.

### Dealing with the massive influx

As Allied forces stormed the beaches of Normandy and eventually pressed inland, breaking the back of the German defensive lines, they scooped up tens of thousands of prisoners.

For security reasons, they could not remain on French soil. So the decision was taken to transport them across the Channel to Britain. Consequently they were herded onto barges, along with wounded Allied soldiers. They would be under strict guard until the barges docked at major southern ports, such as Portsmouth or Southampton.

The German prisoners would then be deloused before being marched to railway stations, where they would board trains to send them to one of the Command Cages for processing.

Command Cages were huge processing centres. One was set up in Lancashire, at the football ground of Preston North End. Others were established at racecourses, such as Catterick or Kempton Park.

It was at these Command Cages that the Prisoner of War Interrogation Section would question the prisoners to see if they had any vital information. They would also be assessed in terms of their political beliefs. On the basis of their answer they would be graded and given a patch to be sewn on their uniform:

- If they were given a white patch they were considered not to be a Nazi, or in fact an anti-Nazi, with no serious political beliefs
- If they were given a grey patch this suggested that they were not ardent supporters of Hitler, but that their political beliefs were questionable
- A black patch was reserved for the fanatical Nazis and automatically any member of the Waffen-SS (fighting SS), Fallschirmjäger (German paratroopers) and U-boat crews. Not all people in this category were necessarily fanatical, but because of their branch of service they were always given a black patch

Other football stadiums, such as Hampden Park, were used as Command Cages. Typically there would be huge rows of tables, where each prisoner was interrogated in turn. They would have to state their:

- Full name
- Rank
- Unit
- And provide proof by showing their papers

Once the interrogators were satisfied, the prisoners would be sent to a delousing station, where they could have a shower or bath. It was likely that the men were then sent onto another location, dependent upon their grading. This could be in another entirely different part of the British Isles. Here they could be given cigarettes and, perhaps, a blanket.

The last thing that the British wanted was to allow hardcore Nazis to mix with regular German soldiers. The screening process did not always work. There was also the problem of what to do with individuals, such as the Polish, who had joined the German army to fight on the Eastern Front, but had actually been captured in France.

### The typical prisoner of war camp

Each of the prisoner of war camps to which all of the men were ultimately sent had a Lagerführer. He would be English-speaking and would act as the liaison officer with the prison guards, as well as trying to instil some discipline amongst the camp inmates.

An important part of this individual's job was also to organise the work details. Prisoners could work if they wanted to and most were involved either in farm work, construction, or clearing up bomb damage. Obviously amongst the German prisoners were huge numbers of skilled workmen and tradesmen and these were pressed into action, particularly in construction.

Incredibly the Germans were paid current union rates of pay. This worked out, for a 48-hour week, as something like three to six shillings a week. But this was not without its problems and there were strikes from British workers, particularly in London. Dockers in Newcastle threatened the same and others even offered to work longer hours rather than have German prisoners of war doing their jobs.

A large letter P was painted on the trouser leg of prisoners of war that were working on repairs or building houses. Around 22,000 German prisoners were engaged in construction alone.

As we will see, the conditions in each of the prisoner of war camps differed. Usually they would be assigned huts, which could house up to 80 men. The camps were well organised, with plenty of recreational facilities. Learning English proved to be extremely popular. As there was a shortage of paper for writing, all sorts of materials were used, such as toilet paper or the labels from tin cans.

The German prisoners were given the same ration allocation per day as serving British soldiers, which was actually more than a civilian's ration.

If a German prisoner was working then he would receive meat, bacon, bread, margarine, plus cheese, tea and vegetables on a weekly basis.

During the Second World War literally hundreds of camps were set up all across Great Britain. It is quite likely that one is close by wherever you are in the country. Of course all of the German prisoners have long since been released, but a considerable number chose to stay in Britain after the war. Perhaps the most bizarre story is that of Hans Teske. He was captured in Tunisia in 1943 and was due to have been repatriated towards the end of 1948. At the time he was living in Buckinghamshire on parole. Somehow his paperwork was either missed or mislaid and he never received his repatriation papers. Despite appealing and even contacting a local MP and the German government he was never put on the repatriation list. In 1970, he finally gave up and so was technically still a German prisoner of war living in Great Britain.

# Chapter Two

# Locations in England

THERE is considerable confusion about the exact number of prisoner of war camps that were used during the Second World War in Great Britain. Certainly it is the case that there were different types of camps used. Some of them were base camps and others were simply hostels. Some of the sites were large, whilst others were smaller, or perhaps only temporary sites. What is also confusing is the fact that the prisoner of war camps were given an official number.

On the face of it this looks fairly straightforward, ranging from 1 to 1026. The problem arises that some camps were allocated two numbers and, on other occasions, a camp number actually refers to several different sites in completely different parts of the country. Other sites simply had an additional letter added to the number.

We can understand why so much of the information remained secret, certainly during the Second World War. There was the understandable fear that the Germans could launch an operation aimed at releasing large numbers of their own men. At the same time the Germans did make requests for location information on the basis that they did not want to accidentally bomb the camps.

Some of the main base camps would have a number of hostels attached to them. Tracing these is incredibly difficult, since records are fragmentary at best. There does appear, however, to be four different types of what could broadly be described as a prisoner of war camp:

- Command Cages – which tended to be in existing buildings and were little more than temporary holding areas for interrogation purposes
- Interrogation Centres – these were more secure units, which were used to carry out long-term debriefings and interrogations of key German personnel
- Transit Camps – these were temporary accommodation, usually tented and designed only for the temporary housing of prisoners of war before they were allocated to a more permanent camp
- Internment Camps or Standard Camps – these would be more permanent and could consist of a tented camp or a purpose-built site with huts, such as Nissen huts, concrete structures or brick buildings

As far as being able to see former prisoner of war camps today, they fall into a number of different categories:

- Some are complete, with virtually all of the structures still in existence, but they may have been converted into civilian use, such as an industrial estate
- Nearly complete, where it is possible to see the overall structure of the camp as more than half of the buildings still exist
- Partial remains, this can cover a wide range of different sites. Some may have a handful of buildings left, whilst others you may just be able to see the main roads or paths that used to run through the camp.
- No remains, which are sites where there is very little sense of what was once a prisoner of war camp. Very little evidence can be seen. This can also mean that traces of the site are probably only visible from the air

**Prisoner of war camps in England**
By 1940, there were 11 prisoner of war camps dotted around the whole of Great Britain, eight of which were in England. These were:

- Grizedale Hall in Lancashire (Camp 1)
- Glen Mill near Oldham in Lancashire (Camp 2)
- Windlestone Hall in County Durham (Camp 4)
- Warth Mills near Bury in Lancashire (Camp 8)
- Kempton Park Racecourse in Surrey (Camp 9)
- Cockfosters in Barnet, London (Camp 10)
- The Hayes, Swanwick, Derbyshire (Camp 13)
- Wilton Park, Beaconsfield, Buckinghamshire (Camp 20)

By November 1942 there were far more camps throughout the British Isles and at this stage they were differentiated into five different categories:

- German
- Italian
- Vichy French
- Invasion camps
- Italian working camps

In each of the following cases, organised by county, we have tried to identify the type of camp and its use, periods of use and its current condition.

## Bedfordshire

### Ducks Cross Camp
Located at Dacca Farm in Wilden, it had been designated as Camp 72. In 1943 the camp had a capacity for housing 750 Italian prisoners, but later it became a standard German working camp.

The prisoners would work on local farms, often with little or no supervision and would be relatively free to involve themselves in the local community.

### WD Camp
It had the designated number of Camp 261 and was at Ampthill. This was a German working camp situated in what is now Ampthill Park. Interestingly, the royal residence and hunting

ground there was used as a prison centuries before, when Henry VIII's first wife, Catherine of Aragon, was held there whilst there were political and legal wrangling about the annulment of their marriage.

### Mansion Potton Camp
Based near Sandy, it was designated as Camp 269. This was a camp with a number of huts and was used as a German working camp, although little else is known about it.

### Luton Airport
Camp 270 was apparently situated at what is now Luton Airport, which was also a German working camp. It is believed that this camp was opened as early as 1940. Towards the end of the war it seems to have reached peak occupancy, with around 3,000 German prisoners of war. It was certainly still operational in 1947.

Looking NW from near to the end of Copt Hall Lane, across the fields of crops towards Luton Airport, where an aircraft can be seen taking off. [*Image courtesy of David P. Howard http://www.geograph.org.uk.*]

According to recent research, the camp itself, consisting of a number of Nissen huts, was based at **Putteridge Bury**, close to the present day airport. Alternatively it may be that the camp was just to the south of **Breachwood Green**. One of the prisoners there was called Erwin Buenger, who was supposedly the personal chauffeur of General Rommel.

### WD Camp
Another WD Camp, this one at Clapham, near Bedford was allocated the number of Camp 278. This is close to Twin Wood airfield, which was opened by the RAF in 1941. This is the airfield where Glenn Miller's aircraft took off on 15th December, 1944 en route to Paris. His aircraft disappeared over the English Channel. There is a Glenn Miller Museum on the site, as well as an Aviation Museum. It is still possible to see some of the buildings that used to belong to the old prisoner of war camp.

### Old Woodbury Hall
Near Gamlingay, it was Camp 561. This building was originally built between 1803 and 1806. During the Second World War it was initially occupied by evacuees and also by troops that had been evacuated from Dunkirk. A small airfield was also constructed here when the RAF moved in. The prisoner of war camp seems to have been situated opposite the main house, although there are no visible remains.

### Church Farm
Church Farm at Marston Moretaine near Bedford had Camp 575. It apparently consisted of a number of Nissen huts but, beyond that, little is known.

### Harrold Hall
Harrold Hall in Harrold was Camp 611. This house was built on the site of a former priory at the beginning of the Seventeenth Century. We know that in the early part of the war it was a barracks for the Pioneer Corps, but, at some point, it became a prisoner of war camp, although very little is known about it.

## Sutton Park

Situated close to Potton, this was Camp 628. This was another camp with a number of Nissen huts as the main housing for the prisoners. Sutton Park had also been used as a prisoner of war camp in the First World War.

The German prisoners were used on local farms. In the First World War, it is believed that the prisoners had been used to remove trees from Sutton Park.

## Berkshire

### Winter Quarter Camp

Winter Quarter Camp in Ascot was designated a special camp and was given the number 7. There is still a good deal of evidence on site, as it is nearly complete. There are a number of guards' huts and there were 26 huts and a football field inside the prisoners' compound. There seems to be some evidence that the camp was used as an internment facility.

The camp was the winter quarters for Bertram Mill's Circus and some of the prisoners were originally housed in the existing buildings, including the elephant houses.

### Lodge Farm

Camp 25 was at Lodge Farm, Baydon, near Newbury. It was initially used for holding Italian prisoners of war. These men tended to work in local agriculture. It later became a German working camp.

### Mortimer Camp

Mortimer Camp, near Stratfield Mortimer was designated as Camp 88. This was a German working camp and it is likely that this camp was open until at least the end of 1948.

### Stanbury House Camp

Based near Reading, it had the designated number of 135. As late as the 1960s there were two Nissen huts that were still standing here, beside Spencers Wood. It is believed that the prisoner of war camp's huts lined the whole driveway. This was apparently a relatively small prisoner of war camp and most of the prisoners worked on local farms. It is believed that a considerable number of these prisoners remained in the area after the war.

### Basildon House

This famous National Trust property near Pangbourne was Camp 246 and lies within Basildon Park. It was built between 1776 and 1783. During the First World War, it had been used as a convalescent hospital. During the Depression years, it was largely abandoned and many of its fixtures and fittings were stripped out. The government again requisitioned it during the Second World War and the area operated as a tank training area, a barracks and, ultimately, a prisoner of war camp. After many more mishaps the property was derelict by 1952 and passed into the hands of the National Trust in 1978, since when it has been extensively restored.

The Palladian Basildon House was home to prisoners of war during the Second World War. [*Image courtesy of Des Blenkinsopp http://www.geograph.org.uk.*]

### Durnell's Farm Camp

Durnell's Farm Camp, near Didcot was Camp 652 and also known as Camp 693.

Originally it was a German working camp. The site is now occupied by Didcot power station.

### Crookham Common Camp

This had the designation number of Camp 1001. We know that this was a former RAF camp and that it became a German working camp. Crookham Common is now perhaps best known for the RAF base that absorbed it, **Greenham Common**. After the Second World War, Greenham Common was used by the US Air Force and although it closed in 1993, it had gained worldwide fame due to the continuing demonstrations and camp outside the perimeter that ran from 1981 to 1993. In fact, the peace camp stayed there until the year 2000.

Interestingly, upwards of 4,000 gliders had been assembled for use on the site by the United States in a variety of glider-borne landings, notably in Normandy and later during Operation Market Garden.

## Buckinghamshire

### Wilton Park Camp

Situated in Beaconsfield, it was designated both as Camp 20 and Camp 300. It was a special camp run by the Combined Services Detailed Interrogation Centre staff. This had originally been established in the Tower of London and then had moved to Trent Park. Because of the increased numbers of prisoners of war, the Wilton Park site and a second at Latimer were established. The main building, a Palladian mansion called the White House, had been built for the former governor of Madras in 1779. This main building was used as the Staff Officers' Mess. The other staff were housed in Nissen huts. The prisoners were in a compound consisting of a number of cells. By the middle of 1943 some fairly high-ranking Germans were taken to the site, including Rudolph Hess. Towards the end of 1945 the Foreign Office took over the centre for denazification purposes of German prisoners. Later it passed to the Army School of Education. The building is still used by the army today.

### Hartwell Dog Track Camp

This camp at Hartwell, near Aylesbury was designated Camp 36. It was used as a prisoner of war camp from 1942 until 1946 and housed mainly Italian soldiers who had been captured in North Africa. Although the prisoners were given some freedom of movement from the camp itself, they were required to wear brown uniforms displaying a large yellow or orange patch on their backs. The camp then became a German working camp and it seems that four separate sites were attached to Camp 36, all of which were opened in August 1945. **Braddenham, Wexham Road** and **Coleshill** were tented camps with a capacity for 100 men, and **Northchurch** was a large hut that could accommodate up to 50 prisoners. By this time, the prisoners would all have been German.

### Shalstone Camp

Located in Shalstone, near Buckingham, it was given the number Camp 55. There is still evidence of several of the original old buildings here. Initially this camp housed Italian prisoners in tents, although these men assisted in the building of concrete housing and were eventually housed in more than 100 huts. Many German prisoners arrived at Shalstone Camp after D-Day and it became a standard type working camp. During this time the camp had a large canteen, a ration storage room and a water tower. It is thought that this camp was finally closed after all the German prisoners had been repatriated in 1949.

### Norduck Farm

Norduck Farm at Aston Abbotts was the site of Camp 153. This is an interesting camp but unfortunately only two of the original Nissen huts still survive. During the Second World War, it was originally used as accommodation for the Czechoslovakian government while they were in exile. By 1945 it had been converted into a prisoner of war camp for German soldiers.

A bridle path leading from Aston Abbotts to Willowbrook Farm crosses this field near to Norduck Farm. The wood straight ahead is Freemasons Wood and some of the Norduck Farm buildings can be seen to the left of this wood. [*Image courtesy of Rob Farrow http://www.geograph.org.uk.*]

### Hitcham Park
It is probable that this German working camp, Camp 684, near Burnham, was centred around a number of huts that were certainly visible in 1946 but had apparently been removed by 1947. There is considerable debate about precisely where this prisoner of war camp was located and two different locations in this small area have been suggested.

## Cambridgeshire

### Barton Field Camp
Camp 26 was a German working camp near Ely, but very little evidence remains of its existence, as the site is now covered with a

golf course and housing. What we do know is that it was capable of holding up to 5,000 prisoners. It was an open camp, with only a minimum amount of guards, so the German soldiers there must have already been screened and designated as relatively low risk.

### Trumpington Camp
Located in Trumpington, it was designated as both Camp 45 and Camp 180. Initially, it housed up to 750 Italian prisoners of war, until at least the end of 1943. After the Normandy landings in June 1944 it was switched to house German prisoners of war and operated as a German working camp. It was still certainly in use post-war, until at least 1947, because a German prisoner of war captured in Normandy was sent to this camp from Canada as part of a denazification process and subsequently married a local Sunday school teacher. After the prisoner of war camp closed in 1947, the site was used to house Polish soldiers.

### Sawtry Camp
It was on Woodwalton Lane and had the number Camp 59. Initially it housed Italian prisoners in wooden huts, with a capacity of nearly 900 prisoners. These prisoners were housed at the camp, in its satellite camp and in various hostels and on local farms. Later the camp became a German working camp.

### Lower Hare Park
Set in Newmarket, it was designated as Camp 71. Very little is known about the camp, apart from the fact that it was situated on London Road.

### Friday Bridge
Located near Wisbech, it had been designated as Camp 90. The site is now the Friday Bridge International Farm Camp. The prisoner of war camp had tents, compounds and garden plots as well as a basic wire fence. The prisoners were paid in vouchers for their agricultural work and like many other camps, the white classified prisoners were allowed to leave the camp whilst the grey and black designated prisoners remained inside and were not released until much later.

### West Fen Militia Camp
West Fen Militia Camp near Ely was Camp 130. Very little appears to remain of this site and none of the structures can be seen.

### Yaxley Farcet Militia Camp
This was designated Camp 279. This was originally used as an assembly point for troops that had been evacuated from Dunkirk. It became a German working camp and later a camp for displaced persons.

### Histon Camp
The camp on Milton Road in Cambridge was Camp 1025. In all likelihood, the remnants of the site lie beneath a science park.

## Cheshire

### Toft Hall Camp
Designated Camp 2, this camp was not opened until 1942, when it was used primarily for Italian prisoners. The camp itself was near Knutsford and, as late as 1947, according to a House of Commons

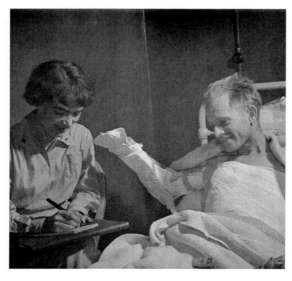

A Red Cross hospital recreation worker in an Army hospital in Great Britain, assisting a soldier whose right arm is in a cast, writing to his relatives back home. [*Image courtesy of Library of Congress Prints and Photographs division 8e02241u.*]

debate, there were over 1,500 prisoners still at the camp, the vast majority of whom were German.

What is interesting is that there were over 30 different nationalities amongst the prisoners, many of whom had fought with the Germans during the war.

This camp was relatively large, with nearly 60 prison huts and the usual double wire fence and guard towers. There is very little evidence left of its existence.

### Number 4 Military Hospital
Located in Knutsford, it was designated Camp 24. This had certainly been a military hospital during the First World War. It is believed that it was primarily used as a secure hospital facility for wounded enemy personnel before they were transferred to other camps.

### Racecourse Camp
The prisoner of war camp, number 74, was situated on the former Tarporley Racecourse in Tarporley. The site was originally used for refugees from Liverpool before it became a German working camp.

### Boar's Head Camp
This was Camp 147, near Nantwich. It was the site of a German working camp and was once also the site of an anti-aircraft battery. There is not a great deal remaining on this site.

### Marbury Hall
Located near Northwich, it was given the designation of Camp 180. Marbury Hall has existed in one form or another since the Thirteenth Century. It once had part of the Parthenon Frieze, which is now in the British Museum. It had a significant art collection, which remained in the hall until around 1932. The building was demolished in 1968. Significantly the British government requisitioned the building in 1940, at that time the building was operating as a country club.

To begin with, it was used as an army camp and housed many men that had been evacuated from Dunkirk. It later became a

German prisoner of war camp and its most famous inmate would later go on to become the goalkeeper for Manchester City. He was a German paratrooper by the name of Bert Trautmann. Trautmann had been transferred to this camp from a transit camp in Essex. He had been designated as a non-Nazi and later transferred to Lancashire, at Camp 50, where he remained until 1948.

### Dunham Park Camp

Camp 189 was at Altrincham and was originally set up for the US Army. The area was inspected initially in September 1942 and, in the following month, the US Army earmarked it, and preparations began. US troops began arriving in October 1943 and they left to prepare for the invasion of Normandy in May 1944.

The camp then became a major base prisoner of war camp, capable of holding up to 3,500 prisoners. Italians began arriving at the beginning of November 1944 and these had been captured in North Africa. However these prisoners of war did not remain in the camp for very long. The Italians that did remain in the camp had considerable problems with the newly arriving German troops. There was a great deal of friction. Polish soldiers guarded the camp.

By 1945, the camp had swelled to 6,000 prisoners of war in around 220 buildings. Many of these were former SS soldiers. Only those that had been screened were allowed to work outside the camp, mainly on farms. We also know that a number of German prisoners of war arrived at the camp from the USA during 1946. The camp was finally closed in late-1948 or early-1949. The majority of the huts were gone by the middle of the 1950s and, today, the camp is part of parkland and woodland. A site where a football pitch was created in a hollow has largely disappeared.

### Crewe Hall

This camp, designated as Camp 191, has a similar story to tell as Dunham Park since it was originally used as an army camp and then a base camp for prisoners of war. The main building is Jacobean and for 30 years was the headquarters of The Wellcome Foundation, although it is now a hotel. At various times during

The long straight drive from Weston Road to Crewe Hall is lined with trees, predominantly birches. [*Image courtesy of Espresso Addict http://www.geograph. org.uk.*]

the Second World War it was used as a training camp, a US Army camp, an operational headquarters and then a prisoner of war camp for German officers (1943).

### Madeley Tile Works Camp
Originally, Italian prisoners of war were housed at Camp 193 in Crewe and then, later, German prisoners began arriving. Many of the Germans remained in the camp until around 1948. Amongst those held at Madeley Tile Works Camp was the German artist Wilhelm Rubenbauer.

### WD Camp at Ledsham Hall
Located near Little Sutton, it was designated Camp 283. This was a German working camp that was mainly tented, with some more permanent buildings.

## Parkgate Camp

Situated in the Wirral and known as Camp 298, little is known about this particular camp.

## Dorfold Hall Camp

Located near Nantwich, it was designated Camp 643. This site has considerable history, as Dorfold Hall is said to have been built on a Saxon site. The current building was constructed in 1616. Initially, the area was used for families that had been bombed out of Liverpool but it later became a US Army base. It's believed that the camp officials and administration were probably housed in the hall and the prisoner of war camp was somewhere within the 18 acres of grounds. The current site is open to the public and is also the home of an annual agricultural show.

## Cornwall

## White Cross Camp

Camp 115 at St Columb Major was originally set up as a prisoner of war camp for Italians but later became a German working camp. The camp was built alongside a railway track and it had a large number of concrete huts and a water tower. It is believed that the camp was capable of housing up to 1,000 men. The Italian prisoners of war built a church but this was later demolished. The area is now a caravan camp but the site of the prisoner of war camp is marked by a monument of an Italian eagle.

## Pennygillam Farm Camp

Camp 257 near Launceston is now an industrial estate. It's believed to have had a very similar history to that of White Cross Camp.

## Scarne Cross Camp

Camp 406 is also near Launceston and was designated Camp 406. It is believed that the site is now covered by an industrial estate and housing.

### Consols Mine Camp
This was designated as Camp 674 and situated near Par.

## County Durham

### Windlestone Hall Camp and Harperley Camp
Windlestone Hall near Rusheyford was a Nineteenth Century country house. It was also the birthplace of Sir Anthony Eden. The whole house and estate were used as a prisoner of war camp, designated Camp 4. It is believed that the camp was probably a satellite of Camp 93 at **Harperley**, near Crook, which was a German working camp.

### Harperley
Camp 93 was purpose-built and was used for low risk prisoners. Initially it housed Italians and by the autumn of 1944 most of the Italians were now in farms and hostels around the area. Nine

The main gate and huts at Harperley prisoner of war camp 93 [*Image courtesy of Rolyat29.*]

The prisoners grew vegetables and also played football at Harperley prisoner of war camp. One of the inhabitants, Bert Trautmann, later became goalkeeper for Manchester City. [*Image courtesy of Rolyat29.*]

The project to make the former Harperley prisoner of war camp a major tourist attraction has stalled due to lack of funds, despite having achieved Ancient Monument status. [*Image courtesy of Alan Murray-Rust http://www. geograph.org.uk.*]

hundred Germans also designated low risk were then sent to Harperley.

**Harperley** (camp 93) was a huge 17-acre camp. It had 50 prison huts, a theatre and a chapel. Many of the buildings still existed into the late 1990s. One of the best-known inmates was Bert Trautmann, who remained in Britain after the war and became Manchester City's goalkeeper. Harperley had a number of subsidiary camps, at Bedburn, Langton Grange, Bishop Auckland, Mount Oswald, Lanchester, Usworth, Hamsterley Hall, Consett and High Spen.
It is believed that one prisoner escaped from this camp and was never recaptured but another routinely escaped, dressing in British uniform, then returning after a night in town.

The camp came up for sale in 1999 and was bought by Lisa and James McLeod. They created a charitable trust in order to preserve the camp and build a museum there. Originally, the camp had

The German prisoners painted the canteen at Harperley with horses and other memories of the German countryside. This image dates from 1946. [*Image courtesy of Rolyat29.*]

about 60 huts and a good number of these still survived. The camp was listed for sale on eBay in 2009 but did not receive any offers. However, in December, 2011, it was announced that English Heritage was donating £500,000 to the camp over a two-year period and that it was hoped the camp would open as a tourist attraction.

### Oaklands
Attached to Camp 93 was an emergency medical centre based at Oaklands in Cockton Hill in Bishop's Auckland. There are a dozen huts that were used during the war and are still in use by the hospital there.

### Walworth Castle
The castle was designated Camp 36. Now a hotel, this Fifteenth Century castle is approximately seven miles to the northwest of Darlington. The castle was used as a prisoner of war camp for

Walworth Castle provided elegant surroundings for high ranking German and Italian prisoner of war officers. [*Image courtesy of Storye Book http://www.geograph.org.uk.*]

200 men. The prisoners were predominantly Italian and later German officers. The camp commandant during the Second World War for Walworth Castle and the Stadium Camp was Major Rollin Holmes. In 1950, Durham County Council bought the castle and it became a girls' boarding school.

During the Second World War, the Durham Light Infantry requisitioned the castle and it was used for high ranking German and Italian prisoner of war officers. In 1950 the Castle was sold to Durham County Council to be made into a residential girls school. It became an hotel in 1981.

### West Boldon Camp

This camp at Down Hill Quarry, Sunderland was Camp 605. We certainly know that Italian prisoners of war were held here and that there were around 16 Nissen huts in use. Little else is known about this site.

### Blackbeck Camp

This was a German working camp at Stainton, designated as Camp 613 and was originally located near a railway line. The British Army used nearby Stainton Camp. It was probably originally an army training camp. We know that many of the Germans that were kept here were captured shortly after the Normandy invasion and also that some of the Germans did not return to Germany after the war. This was because their homes were now in the Russian occupied zone.

### Wolviston Hall

The hall near Billingham was demolished in 1966 and it appears that nothing remains of the site of the prisoner of war Camp 139.

### Coxhoe Hall Camp

This was another country house that was demolished in the post-war period, this time in 1952. Originally designated as Camp 139B, the government requisitioned it in 1939 and all that is known is that it became a prisoner of war camp, first for Italians and then for Germans.

## Cumbria

### *Grizedale Hall*

Grizedale Hall was officially designated Camp 1. It was constructed in the grounds of a 40-roomed mansion, close to the village of Satterthwaite. The building itself had been built in 1903. The Forestry Commission currently owns the site, and the house itself was demolished in 1957. The camp is believed to have consisted of around 30 huts and had a double perimeter wire fence around it, along with watchtowers.

The Grizedale Hall site is best known for the escape of Oberleutnant Franz von Werra. This pilot had been shot down over Kent on 5th September, 1940. He was interrogated and then sent

The last remnants of Grizedale Hall, a glorious building in the heart of the Grizedale Forest, used as a German prisoner of war camp during the Second World War, and setting for the POW film *The One That Got Away,* starring Hardy Kruger. [*Image courtesy of Andy Davis http://www.geograph.org.uk.*]

to Grizedale. He escaped on 7th October and after a period of freedom was recaptured and then attempted to escape again, this time from Swanwick camp in Derbyshire. Again he was recaptured and shipped off to Canada. Here, in transit, he escaped once more and slipped into the United States, which at that time was neutral. The pilot did not survive the war, however. Having been smuggled back to Germany, his Me 109 crashed into the sea off Holland on 25th October, 1941.

Grizedale Hall also held high ranking German officers, including von Rundstedt. At one stage, it also held 50 or so French officers from the Vichy forces that had been captured on Madagascar.

### Moota Camp
Camp number 103 was Moota Camp, near Cockermouth. This was a relatively large facility, with as many as 1,200 prisoners of war, mainly working on neighbouring farms. The site is now a hotel.

### Shap Wells
This camp has two camp numbers, 13 and 15. The main building, Shap Wells, was opened in 1833 to house visitors to Shap Spa. It was a fashionable resort, visited by guests such as HRH Princess Mary. During the Second World War it was used primarily as a camp for more senior German naval and Luftwaffe officers. The site is still operating as a country hotel.

### Merry Thought Camp
This was designated as Camp 76 and was near Calthwaite. This was a German working camp and there are still considerable numbers of buildings on the site today. These are prefabricated huts and there are also concrete imprints of foundations. It was originally occupied by Italians and then subsequently by Germans. Both groups worked on local farms.

### Beela (aka Bela) River Camp
Located near Milnthorpe, it was designated as Camp 104, and listed as a German working camp but housed Italian prisoners of

Built as a prisoner of war camp in the Second World War, Wings School (Beela Camp) site is now used as a boarding school for children with emotional and behavioural difficulties. [*Image courtesy of David Gruar http://www.geograph. org.uk.*]

war before then. There is an interesting little story that one of the British guards of the camp was taken ill and an Italian prisoner patrolled the camp himself with the guard's rifle until a replacement arrived.

### Hornby Hall
The hall in Brougham was Camp 155. There were around 25 Nissen huts here. Some foundations can still be seen in the woodland, although the main site is now a country house hotel.

### No 4 Camp
Located at Longton, near Carlisle, the precise location of Camp 692 has not been identified, although it is known that it was a German working camp.

### Warwick Camp

Warwick Camp, Carlisle was Camp 696. The site was almost certainly a British Army camp, but it is now hidden underneath an industrial estate.

## Derbyshire

### The Hayes

Camp 13 was The Hayes, Swanwick, and was also designated Camp 58, 179 and 297. It was almost certainly a large German working camp with large numbers of tents and huts, wire fences and guard towers.

Franz von Werra of the Luftwaffe escaped from Swanwick and was recaptured trying to steal an aircraft on RAF Hucknall.

The site of the camp was probably based around Swanwick Hall, which had been built in the 1850s. It has been a conference centre for nearly 100 years, which is its main use today.

### Oaks Green

Camp 23, also known as Camp 1023, was at Oaks Green. It was a military hospital and then was converted into a prisoner of war camp. The site is now a prison.

### Nether Heage Camp

Situated on a 14-acre site near Belper, Camp 58 housed what is believed to be approximately 1,4000 Italian prisoners of war who worked as farm labourers locally and at the nearby flax factory. The former prisoner of war camp is now a caravan park.

### New Drill Hall

Clay Cross was Camp 248. This building was originally associated with the Sherwood Foresters who were using it before the First World War. The Sherwood Foresters were created when the 45th Nottinghamshire Regiment and the 95th Derbyshire Regiment were merged in 1881. The site is now occupied by an industrial estate, nothing remains of the prisoner of war camp.

### Alvaston Camp
Designated as Camp 634, it was also listed as Camp 1008. The camp, situated in Meadow Lane, Alvaston is now believed to be the home of a caravan camp.

### Weston Camp
This site at Weston-on-Trent was designated Camp 634 and Camp 635. There is some confusion about the designation of this camp, as the whole area seems to have originally been covered by a large army camp. This was predominantly used for training purposes. At some point the area became a centre for a German working company and it is believed that there was an area sectioned off by a wire perimeter fence.

### No 1 Camp
Located at Oak's Green in Sudbury, it was given the designation Camp 1004, although it is strongly linked with Camp 23 and Camp 1023. These were originally military hospitals, although a German company operated from No 1 Camp.

## Devon

### Bickham Camp
Based near Yelverton, it had the number of Camp 20. It is thought that this was a tented site and consisted of five enclosures, with watchtowers. There is very little to be found today on the site to identify the camp's original design.

### Exhibition Field Camp
The camp at Holsworth was designated as Camp 42 and is now the site of Stanhope Close. It initially housed Italian prisoners, but later became a standard type German working camp. The Church of St Peter in Holsworth has examples of the craftsmanship of some of the prisoners of this camp. There are two hand-painted windows that Italian prisoners made by extracting dye from clothing and vegetables. The windows became part of the hut that the Italian prisoners used as their church in 1942. These were

donated to the church in 1994. In addition, when one of the German prisoners of war was repatriated, the church was presented with his hand-carved crucifix, which now hangs above the altar.

### Dymond's Farm
The farm at Clyst Honiton was designated as Camp 76.

### Bampton Road Camp
A school now stands on the site of the original camp near Tiverton, designated as Camp 92.

### Hazeldene Camp
The camp near Plymstock was designated Camp 137. It was also known as Elburton Camp, due to the fact that the prisoner of war camp was just to the east of Elburton. Italians were first housed there, where they converted a barn into a chapel. Unfortunately this no longer exists. The Italians and later the Germans were used to work on local farms and clearing bomb damage in Plymouth. They were identified by wearing brown uniforms with multicoloured patches. The Germans and also Austrians were used until at least 1946 for building work. It is believed that the majority of the men began leaving the camp at the beginning of May 1948. Many of them were bound for a transit camp in Suffolk.

### Chaddlewood Camp
Chaddlewood Camp was also designated Camp 137. This may have simply been part of the larger overall prison camp structure in the area. Five of the German prisoners of war married local women.

### Winsford Towers Camp
Located near Beaworthy, it was designated Camp 137B. The government set up railway sidings here in 1943 and the United States had a large camp here prior to the D-Day landings. Also around this time there was a camp for Italian prisoners of war, although the exact location is unknown.

This former mansion house was originally set in extensive parkland, which also contained Chaddlewood Farm. It was used as a prisoner of war camp during the Second World War and it is now divided into retirement apartments. [*Image courtesy of Nigel Mole http://www.geograph.org.uk.*]

### Nissen (aka Nisson) Camp
Camp 276 was at Nissen or Nisson Camp at Pinhoe, near Exeter, and was a German prisoner of war camp.

### Country House Hotel
The camp at Sidford near Sidmouth was designated Camp 598. It's believed that this is the present location of the Sid Valley Country House Hotel.

### Bridestow Camp
Very little remains of Camp 673 near Oakhampton on Dartmoor and it is now just woodland.

### Home Park Camp
Also designated Camp 673 was Home Park Camp near Plymouth. This was a German working camp. Its precise location is unknown,

but it is interesting that this is also the name of the ground of Plymouth Argyll Football Club. Like most of the football stadiums, it was closed during the war years, and it was bombed. We know that, when the ground was reopened in 1945, army huts were used as changing rooms, so it is possible that German prisoners of war were temporarily housed there.

### Cruwys Morchard
Camp 669 was near Tiverton in North Devon.

### Bradninch Camp
This was a German working camp near Exeter that was probably centred around a farm and was designated Camp 1022.

### Ivybridge Camp
The camp near Ivybridge had the designation of Camp 404 and also Camp 187. It is likely that this camp occupied a site that was demolished in the 1970s and a school and housing have since been built there. We know that this operated as a base camp for some time.

### Handy Cross Camp
This German working camp near Bideford and designated Camp 694, was built on the site of an existing British Army camp.

## Dorset

### Motcombe Park Camp
Designated as Camp 47, it was situated on the west field of Motcombe House near Shaftesbury. After repatriation the camp was used for displaced persons before it became the home of the Port Regis School.

### Cattistock Camp
Located near Dorchester, it was designated Camp 295. It seems that the Cattistock Camp was used as a central base area for a number of other camps containing Italian and German prisoners of war

who tended to work on farms. The sub-camps controlled by Cattistock had between 25 and 150 prisoners.

### Park Camp

Camp 688 was Park Camp at West Lulworth. The British Army set up a camp here in February 1918. However, the site itself had been used as an impromptu camp during the Nineteenth Century. The prisoner of war camp is marked as a German working camp, believed to have been situated in woodland.

### Merley Park Camp

Sited near Wimborne Minster, it had Camp 1021 as its designated number. This was an existing British Army camp and some of the South Wales Borderers were sent there in December, 1942. It almost certainly became a camp for American troops before being transformed into a German working camp. U-boat crews were also held at this camp. It is believed that the site of the camp now contains caravans and used to house Merley Bird Gardens.

## Essex

### High Garrett Camp

Camp 78, near Braintree was originally an Italian prisoner of war camp, housing around 200 men. Later, this became a German working camp. The site, formerly RAF High Garrett, is marked by a radio mast and is now a crematorium.

### Mill Lane Camp

Situated on Mill Lane, which was a cul-de-sac near Hatfield Heath, it was Camp 116. The current site is known as Camp Farm. It is believed that the majority of the original buildings have now been cleared and the current site is used as an egg packing station.

### Ashford Camp

Near Halstead, it had the designation of Camp 129. Ashford Lodge was used as an American Army Ordnance Depot. Initially, Italian prisoners were housed here, then it became a German working camp. The local Rotary Club at Braintree was involved in educating prisoners of war in Ashford Camp and a number of the prisoners remained in the area and later became British citizens.

### Radwinter North Camp
Located at Radwinter Manor, Radwinter was Camp 180. When the war started, this was the site of Radwinter Rectory and it later became Radwinter Manor. One of the German prisoners of war was Karl Weschke, a noted artist. He had joined the Luftwaffe and became a paratrooper in 1942 and was taken prisoner in Holland. He remained in Britain after the war and lived on Cape Cornwall, near Land's End for over 40 years. He died in 2005. As for the camp itself, very little remains apart from some imprints of the hut complexes in fields.

### Berechurch Hall Camp
Based near Colchester, it was given the number of Camp 186. This is now a military corrective training centre and part of the greater complex of army buildings around the Colchester area. More modern army buildings have now replaced the hut complex, with its standard wire perimeter fence, although it is believed that some of the original huts do still exist.

### White House Camp
This was on Church Hill in Loughton and was designated Camp 236. The site of the prisoner of war camp is probably now covered with housing. There's an urban myth that the Loughton camp area was one of the places that Boadicea made her last stand against the Romans. That said, it is a scheduled ancient monument and contains a hill fort.

### Bentley Farm
Bentley Farm, Old Church Hill, Langdon Hills was Camp 266 and was a German working camp. It was probably a former army camp before it became a prisoner of war camp. The site of the camp is likely to be close to Dry Street, on a flat piece of land. Until

relatively recently, there was at least one concrete pad of one of the huts remaining.

## Purfleet Camp

Located at Beacon Hill, near Purfleet, it had the designation Camp 286. This site area has been used for many years as an army camp. There was an anti-aircraft battery there during the First World War and a musketry camp close by that was open between 1914 and 1961. The prisoner of war camp was also designated the number 654, or No 4 Transit Camp, and 655, No 1 Transit Camp. We know that the prisoners were housed in tents but there was a more permanent collection of huts, which were probably the original camp for guards. There was also a wire enclosure around the site.

## Ickleton Grange

Camp 607 was Ickleton Grange in Ickleton. Aerial photographs of Ickleton Grange reveal the presence of long Nissen huts. These were situated close to the main building. There are also clear signs of the imprint of a number of other buildings alongside Grange Road.

## Shaftesbury Camp

Located in Dovercourt, near Harwich, Shaftesbury Camp was Camp 670B, but it was also known as Camp 680. The site operated as a German working camp but also Harwich was a major exit port for repatriation. It had been decided in June, 1948 to send back around 10,000 of the German prisoners of war that were still working in Britain. Repatriations would begin in the November. It was planned that some 800 Germans each day would be sent to Harwich by train and there were serious concerns that many of the men would not want to go back.

## Gloucestershire

## Sudeley Castle Camp

Based in Winchcombe, it was designated Camp 37. The castle has a history dating back to the Romans and was the former home of

Sudeley Castle housed both prisoners of war and important works of art during the Second World War. [*Image courtesy of Michael Reeve.*]

Katherine Parr, the surviving wife of Henry VIII. Katherine Parr is buried in the grounds of the castle. Initially Italian prisoners of war were held at the camp at Sudeley Castle, working on local farms. They were given a degree of freedom but were enforced to wear brown battledress uniforms with a white ring on the back to identify them as prisoners of war. The camp was sited in the grounds of the castle and later became a German working camp. During the war, Sudeley Castle also became a safe house for the Tate Gallery's picture collection, which was stored there to protect it from damage during the London Blitz.

### Wynols Hill
Wynols Hill, Broadwell, Coleford, or Camp 61, housed around 750 Italian prisoners in 1942, but the camp had grown in size by the

following year and housed 950 Italian prisoners. In December, 1944 the Italian prisoners unveiled a memorial they had built to commemorate Marconi and the 50th anniversary of radio transmissions. The men had built the memorial from anything they could find, but sadly it fell into disrepair and had to be demolished in the late 1970s. The camp is now the site of a housing estate.

### Sedbury

The camp at Sedbury was not given a listed number, as was the case with many camps around Great Britain. The site at Sedbury had been a prisoner of war camp during the First World War and during the Second World War the camp had 30 huts within a gated perimeter fence, guard towers and a recreation ground, as well as laid out gardens. After repatriation of the prisoners the site was used as housing for ex-servicemen.

Remains of the camp at Sedbury in Gloucestershire. [*Image courtesy of Nicholas Mutton, http://www.geograph.org.uk.*]

## Wapley Camp

Wapley Camp, Yate, near Bristol (now in South Gloucestershire) was Camp 124. It housed Italian prisoners of war until at least the end of 1944.

## Ashton Gate and Bedminster Camps

Ashton Gate Camp was designated Camp 124 and there was also Bedminster Camp, which was designated Camp 124A. Both of these were also in Bristol. We know these latter camps operated as German working camps. Post-war, the camps around Bristol became centres for displaced Polish troops.

## Northwick Park Hospital

Northwick Park Hospital was in Blockley and called Camp 132. This is now housing and a business centre. The camp was centred round the original Northwick Park Mansion. We certainly know that the park area was an American field hospital during the Second World War and that it later became a camp for displaced Poles. The camp, originally the 327th Station Hospital, was manned by US medical staff. It was used to treat many injured German prisoners of war. The hospital closed in June, 1945.

## Bourton Camp

Camp 157 was Bourton Camp at Bourton-on-the-Hill. This was a large base camp, with at least six compounds containing prisoner of war huts. It seems that this was a relatively high security unit, as there were two bands of wire perimeter fencing and watchtowers. The site is now forest and we also know that after the war the prisoner of war camp became a Polish refugee camp.

## Spring Hill

Camp 185 was at Spring Hill, near Blockley and operated as a camp for displaced persons until it was closed in 1958. The majority of the refugees here were Polish. The camp covered around seven acres, with a wide range of accommodation huts, plus a chapel, a canteen and a cinema. Most of the camp still exists.

Some of the huts that were used to house German prisoners of war were pulled down shortly after the end of the Second World War but there are still some concrete foundations visible.

### Leckhampton Court Camp
Camp 263 was located in Leckhampton, near Cheltenham. This is a medieval manor house, which had been requisitioned during the First World War as a hospital and then again in 1939. Originally it housed the Durham Light Infantry. In 1942, the US Army Signal Corps troops used the site. One of the men working for the US Signal Corps at nearby Benhall which was billeted in Leckhampton Court was Mickey Rooney.

By 1945 the court became a working camp for German prisoners of war. They tended to work on local farms and later helped to refurbish the Parish hall.

### Northway Camp
Northway Camp, Ashchurch was designated as Camp 1009. The Ministry of Defence occupies the general area of the site to this day and uses it as a vehicle storage area. However, during the Second World War, Northway was a German working camp, with a perimeter fence and watchtowers. Many of the original buildings have now been demolished and some of the original site may now have post-war housing.

## Hampshire

### Anglesey House
Anglesey House at Hoath End, near Aldershot was designated Camp 30.

### Ganger Camp
Ganger Camp in Romsey was designated Camp 41. It was a standard German working camp and once the prisoners had all been repatriated, their huts were taken over by the local council. The huts housed local residents until they could be replaced by new housing. Little remains of the original prisoner of war camp.

### Setley Plain Camp
Based at Brockenhurst in the New Forest, this was Camp 65. Initially housing Italians who had been captured in North Africa, the camp later became a standard type German working camp. The prisoners worked in the New Forest, and the camp, which finally closed during the 1960s, was then used to house homeless people after the prisoners had been repatriated.

### East Cams Camp
Camp 251 was East Cams Camp at Portchester Road, Fareham. This was a German working camp and modern housing probably now hides the site.

### Fisher's Camp
Camp 294 was Fisher's Camp at Theddon Grange near Alton. This is a former country house that has now been split up into a number of flats and houses. It served as a German working camp.

### Southampton Common
Camp C19 was at 402A, The Avenue on Southampton Common. The reason for the strange designation of this camp was that this was originally a D-Day marshalling area camp. It would have almost certainly been tented accommodation, which was swiftly switched over for use as a prisoner of war camp and was possibly only ever intended to be a temporary camp.

### Carfax Estate
Based at Tongham, it was designated as Camp 584.

### Stoneham Camp
Situated in Eastleigh and designated as Camp 614, this camp was to the northeast of Eastleigh airport. In all probability, this was also the site of a camp that was set up to house refugee Basque children in 1937.

### Ossemsley Manor
Camp 624 was at Ossemsley Manor, New Milton. The camp was used by troops of the British 56th Infantry Brigade shortly before they left for Normandy. At that stage, it had triple barbed wire perimeter fencing and large, square American tents. The men were shifted out of the camp towards the end of May, 1944. The camp subsequently became a holding area for German prisoners of war.

### Arena Road Camp
Camp 632 in Tidworth was located close to or was a part of Tidworth Barracks. By early-1948, the camp had been closed and displaced persons were housed there.

### Haig Lines
Camp 633 was Haig Lines in Crookham. This extensive camp was begun in 1914 but most of it was built in the late-1930s for the Royal Army Medical Corps. It had an extensive area of huts and more substantial buildings. The site was a German working camp.

### Quarr House
Set in the New Forest at Sway, Lymington, Quarr House was designated Camp 645. At one point early in the Second World War, a Canadian tank regiment was based there, but the prisoner of war camp at that time was probably situated a couple of miles away at Setley Plain, near Brockenhurst. Quarr House initially housed Italian prisoners of war and then Germans. Some of the prisoners worked at a local sawmill.

### Park House A
Park House in Shipton Bellinger, Tidworth was Camp 663. Australian troops were billeted in the Tidworth area in 1940. Australians had also been at Park House camp during the First World War, housed in a huge, tented camp. It is believed that there was a German working camp here during the Second World War.

### Fargo Camp

Fargo Camp, Larkhill near Salisbury was Camp 672. This became a Polish resettlement camp in 1946 but, before that, it had a long army tradition. A tented camp was set up there in 1899 and the first permanent huts built in 1914. Some 34 garrisons of battalion size were built in the area during the First World War alone. The whole area was extended again during the Second World War when it was a German working camp and the former site is now occupied by housing.

### Hiltingbury Road

Based in Chandler's Ford, near Eastleigh, it was designated as Camp 675. The Hiltingbury woods area was used as a concentration point for around 10,000 Allied troops in the latter stages of the preparations for the D-Day landings. After they had departed for France, the area became a prisoner of war camp. Later, it became a camp for Polish dependents.

### Puckridge Camp

The German working camp was designated as Camp 676 and was in Fleet Road, Aldershot.

### Whitchurch Camp

Camp 693A was Whitchurch Camp on Newbury Road, Whitchurch. This was a small hostel that was used to house German prisoners of war.

### Oakhanger

Oakhanger, Bordon was Camp 1000. This area has a long association with the British Army and there were many camps in the local area. A large, hutted camp was built near Oxney Farm. We know that the Bordon area was occupied by British and Canadian troops. The actual German prisoner of war camp, which had initially been occupied by Canadians until the latter stages of the Second World War, was Lower Oakhanger Camp. This was situated near a level crossing in Station Road. After it had ceased to be used as a prisoner of war camp, it was used by

European Volunteer Workers, who remained there until the 1950s.

### Willems Barracks

This was designated Camp 1006 and was at Aldershot. This was originally known as the West Cavalry Barracks and had been constructed in the 1850s. British cavalry regiments were housed there until 1938. As the camp contained guardrooms and cells, as well as other substantial buildings, it was pressed into action as a prisoner of war camp. The area is now occupied by housing and a large retail store.

### Beaumont Barracks

This was also at Aldershot and was designated as Camp 1019. In all likelihood this was a similar situation to that of Willems Barracks. We know that the barrack blocks themselves were demolished in 1975. The original buildings were built in the 1850s

The old army sheds at what is now Moreton business park. [*Image courtesy of Whatlep, http://www.geograph.org.uk.*]

and all that now remains is a guardroom, the main wall, some cells and a riding school.

## Herefordshire

### Moreton-on-Lug Camp

This was designated as Camp 686. There was certainly a US Army ordnance depot and medical depot at Moreton-on-Lug, which had a capacity of some 1,500 men. It appears that this may have been another instance where a camp post-June 1944 became a German working camp.

## Hertfordshire

### Batford Camp

This was an Italian prisoner of war camp that was opened in the summer of 1943 near Harpenden. Initially, it consisted of tents, then huts were added. The site was designated Camp 95 and it appears that it was still in operation until at least 1947. By November, 1944, the Italians had been moved into hostels and the camp then housed at least 750 Germans. The repatriation of the German prisoners of war had been accomplished by July, 1948. Local satellite hostels, which had been used successfully for the Italian prisoners of war were also later used with the Germans, at Hatfield Hyde, Lemsford and Stanborough.

### Ledbury Camp

Camp 27 was Ledbury Camp, which is now occupied by the John Masefield School, itself constructed in the 1950s. Camp 27 operated as a German working camp.

### Royston Heath Camp

Camp 29 was Royston Heath Camp and was a purpose-built working camp that opened in 1941 and remained operational until 1948. There are some concrete foundations, holes from posts and other evidence still in existence.

### 33 Dancer's Hill Camp

Located at South Mimms, it was designated Camp 33 and contained huts and tents. It was encircled by a double wire perimeter fence and had a small satellite tented camp to the southwest of it.

### Meesden

German working camp near Buntingford was designated Camp 128.

### Gorhambury Park

This camp for German prisoners, near Hemel Hempstead, was designated as Camp 235.

### Arches

These was a second camp close by, also designated Camp 235, which was the Arches at Felden. The camp was initially a training centre for the Women's Land Army. It was later transformed into a German working camp. Interestingly, Felden is the national headquarters of the Boys' Brigade.

### Wynches Camp

Wynches Camp, Much Hadham was Camp 411. This was originally a training camp and the Ghurkhas and American troops were housed there. Once these men had moved to mainland Europe, it became a German working camp.

In September, 2010, David Murray, a local, was gardening and he discovered a dog tag. Over the next few months, he unearthed 2,000 objects, including bottles and padlocks, as well as identity tags. It transpires that Wynches Camp held both Italian and German prisoners of war and that it extended over 40 acres. It was used as a major camp and up to 10,000 prisoners of war were held there. There is now housing and parkland on the site.

## Kent

### *Shorncliffe Camp*
This was designated both as Camp 33 and Camp 670a. It was situated on St Martin's Plain in Cheriton, a suburb of Folkestone and had formerly been a military camp. The British Army used the area regularly for manoeuvres and training.

### *Somerhill Camp*
Based near Tonbridge, Somerhill Camp was designated Camp 40. It is believed that the camp spanned two roads on the Somerhill estate and was used from 1940 until 1945 with a capacity of 40 huts of varying size in a barbed wire enclosure. Initially it housed captured Italians but later German prisoners who had been shot down were kept there in a working camp. By 1948, Somerhill was being used as temporary housing for those made homeless by the bombing during the Blitz.

### *Woodchurch Camp*
Woodchurch Camp, near Ashford, had the designation of Camp 86 but it is also listed as Honghorst House and Camp 282 and also listed as Hengherst. It is likely that the prisoners of war were billeted in farm buildings, as the house itself was not built until after the Second World War.

### *Walderslade Camp*
This was in King George Street, Chatham and designated Camp 117. This suburb of Chatham housed a German working camp. It was situated on Hook Meadow and it seems that the majority of the men had already been screened and were considered either non-political or anti-Nazi. Many of them also carried out voluntary work in local residents' gardens. There is also some suggestion that Walderslade originally housed Italian prisoners of war. There were still some traces of the camp as late as 1951 but the camp itself closed in June 1948.

### Ministry of Works Camp

Camp 154 was called the Ministry of Works Camp and was in Swanscombe Street, Swanscombe. It was a German working camp and the site is now covered with modern housing.

### Summer House

Camp 233 was at Summer House, near Ravensbourne. This is now a school, which celebrated its 100th anniversary in 2011. In 1944, part of the school was evacuated and there was a German working camp in the grounds towards the end of the war and beyond.

### Coed-Bel Camp

Coed-Bel Camp on Lubbock Road, Chislehurst, was designated as Camp 237. Coed-Bel was opened as a school in 1877 by its headmistress, Katherine Amos. It was used as a hospital during the First World War between October 1914 and March 1919. The school was evacuated in 1941 and the site is listed as a German working camp.

### Mereworth Castle

Camp 267 was Mereworth Castle in Mereworth. This is not so much a castle but a country house that was built on the site of a fortified manor house. It was used as a German working camp during the Second World War and subsequently changed hands several times. It is now owned by a former ambassador of the United Arab Emirates.

### Brissenden Green Camp

Situated at Brissenden near Ashchurch, it was designated Camp 282.

### Mabledon Camp

This was in Mabledon Park, near Tonbridge and was designated as Camp 629. Mabledon Park was one of a number of D-Day transit camps that were occupied by the Canadian Army before it was transformed into a prisoner of war camp for Germans. A school occupies the site of this former camp.

### Royal Engineers Bridging Camp

This was at Wouldham, near Rochester and was designated as Camp 654A. The site has a long association with the Royal Engineers, and the Royal Marines also used it when they trained for a raid on Zeebrugge in the First World War. The site had a number of compounds; amongst which was a detention barracks. It was also used as a German working camp.

### St Radigund's Camp

Based near Dover, it was known as Camp 670. This area, near Buckland Hospital, was named after an abbey, which in turn was named after a German princess. It became a German working camp. There were several camps in the area, including one at Tilmanstone which housed Italian prisoners who worked on the farms, some of whom married local girls.

## Lancashire

### Glen Mill

This was in Oldham and is variously designated as Camp 2, 168 and 176. It was a disused cotton mill with a number of weaving sheds and other buildings. It was generally used as a transit camp for German prisoners that were destined for Canada. Later in the war, it was also used to house large numbers of Russians who had been fighting in the German armed forces and been captured in France.

It is believed that the camp was a relatively large one and could hold between 2,000 and 5,000 prisoners. There were a number of escape attempts made from this prison. Most of them failed, but the handful that was successful was quickly recaptured. There is an unconfirmed story of two German prisoners of war actually making a successful home run and it is said that they sent a rather unpleasant letter to the camp commandant from Hamburg.

Glen Mill was opened in the late autumn of 1939 and closed in September 1947.

## Warth Mills

Camp 8 was Warth Mills, a former cotton mill in Bury. This camp was also designated Camp 9, 12A and 177. There are limited remains of the camp here and it seems that it was used as a transit camp for Italian prisoners of war en route to the Isle of Man.

## Ormskirk

At Ormskirk, there are significant remains of what was Camp 29, which was operational between 1942 and 1945. There seems to have been a number of workshops in operation there and some evidence of the original buildings can still be found amongst the woodland and undergrowth.

## Garswood Park

The camp near Ashton-in-Makerfield, in the borough of Wigan, initially housed around 800 Italian prisoners but was later used as a standard-type German working camp. Garswood Park camp closed in 1948 and the few remaining Germans who had not been repatriated were transferred to Dunham Park Camp near Altrincham in Cheshire (Camp 189). Today, the site is occupied by two schools.

## Bank Hall Camp

Bank Hall Camp at Bretherton, near Preston, was designated as Camp 65. The Jacobean hall was the billet of the Royal Engineers during the Second World War. There is evidence of the former German working camp to the southeast of the hall. The remains of the huts are scattered in woodland.

## Melland Camp

This was designated as Camp 126 and was located on Sandfold Lane, Gorton near Manchester. This was the site of an anti-aircraft battery and, later, a German working camp.

## Newton Camp

Based at Newton with Scales near Kirkham, this was Camp 146. This German working camp was close to the RAF camp at

Kirkham and was originally the site of a searchlight unit. The first enemy arrivals were Italians, who worked locally on farms.

### Brook Mill Camp
This base camp was also near Kirkham and designated Camp 168.

### Camp A
Camp A, at Knowsley Park, near Prescot, was also known as Camp 171. The area around Huyton was used extensively as a base for several prisoner of war camps. There was also an internment camp there, where large numbers of individuals, some of whom were refugees from Germany, were scooped up. The whole area was secure and the first camp, which was opened in May 1940, was set in unfinished council houses and flats, surrounded by rubble. The majority of the internees were released before the internment camp was closed in 1942. The prisoner of war camp is thought to have closed in 1948.

### Penketh Hostel
Located on South Lane Farm, Barrows Green, this was Camp 290. This was the site of a heavy anti-aircraft battery and there was a camp alongside the battery which was converted into a German working camp. Parts of the camp can just be seen alongside Farnworth Road.

### Fort Crosby
Fort Crosby at Sniggery Farm, Hightown was Camp 678. This is northwest of an area called Sniggery Wood, to the east of the railway line that runs from Liverpool to Southport. It was a German working camp that was in use until 1948. The camp probably occupied an old coastal battery and anti-aircraft battery and associated buildings. Very little is left amongst the sand dunes.

## Leicestershire

### Scraptoft
Based near Thurnby, it was designated Camp 4. Towards the end of the war, it was used as a repatriation camp.

### Gaulby Billesdon

There are few remains of a German working camp, designated Camp 94, which was situated on Gaulby Billesdon. Most of the site is now wooded land, although there is a sign and a basic map that identifies the positions of the concrete bases of the prisoner of war huts. A single hut remains, showing the basic structure.

### Quorn Camp

Camp 9 was Quorn Camp on Wood Lane, Quorn. It was also designated Camp 183 and was a standard prisoner of war camp or base camp. Aerial photography can clearly pick out the footprints of the camp buildings. This site was initially used as the main camp for the US paratroopers and was used as a prisoner of war camp after these troops had been deployed in Normandy. When the prisoners left, the Royal Leicestershire and Royal Lincolnshire Regiments moved in at different times, with the camp eventually closing in 1959 to revert to farmland.

### Garendon Park and Knighthorpe Camp

Camp 28 was at Garendon Park, Loughborough. The camp may have been centred around Garendon Hall, which was used for troop accommodation during the Second World War. The original building was demolished in the 1960s.

Camp 28 was also known as Knighthorpe Camp and was a German working camp.

### Farndon Road and Harrington Camps

This was situated on Farndon Fields Farm near Market Harborough. This camp was designated Camp 49 and was also known as Harrington Camp. This was a standard type German working camp and, today, is the home of a caravan site.

### Old Liberal Club

Based on Charnwood Road, Shepshed, it was Camp 152. This is now a rest home and it was built at the beginning of the Twentieth Century, officially being known as Charnwood Hall. It was used as a German working camp.

### Shady Lane

Camp 167 was on Shady Lane in Stoughton and there were German prisoners of war at this camp until 1948. They worked on the land, as well as helping to build roads and sewers in Leicester.

### Hathern Camp

Hathern Camp in Pear Tree Lane, Hathern was designated Camp 590. This site is now occupied by housing and farmland.

### Old Dalby Camp

The camp was a large, hutted collection of buildings in Old Dalby Lane, Melton Mowbray with the number Camp 613. In the 1930s, unemployed men would carry out heavy labour in Dalby Forest. The camp operated until about 1939 and there was already an instructional centre there. The prisoner of war camp was associated with an RAF depot located in the area.

### Barkby Camp

This was designated as Camp 616 and was in Barkby Lane, Leicester. At one stage, there was an anti-aircraft battery here, but, in 1942, it began to be used as an area for Italian prisoners of war. There were vestiges of the camp still in existence in 2011, which were mentioned in a conservation area appraisal.

## Lincolnshire

### Stamford Camp

Situated on Empingham Road, this was designated both Camp 10 and Camp 106. There were a number of prefabricated buildings on the site, which were later converted to civilian post-war use. There is now more modern housing on this site.

### Allington

Camp 51 was at Allington, near Grantham and had a capacity of 750 prisoners during the time the Italians were incarcerated there. By 1946, however, more than 1,000 German prisoners were in the camp, which was a standard working camp. The camp closed as a prisoner of war camp in 1947 and then became a transit camp for displaced persons. The site is now occupied by housing.

## Nether Headon Camp

Formerly in Lincolnshire, but now in Nottinghamshire, the site of Nether Headon Camp, designated Camp 52, is now an industrial estate. The prisoner of war camp was a standard type German working camp.

## Moorby Camp

Moorby Camp near Ravensby was Camp 79 and, until fairly recently, was listed by English Heritage as being one of only five intact prisoner of war camps in England. The camp was being used to rear turkeys for a number of years. We know that it was a German working camp that was in use until 1948. Many of the buildings are still there, although there has been some destruction in recent years.

## Horbling Camp

This German working camp near Sleaford was originally Camp 80. The site is now virtually obliterated as it is covered with housing. The camp was still in operation until 1948 and was a fully equipped, purpose-built camp. Most of the prisoners worked as labourers on local farms.

## Pingley Farm Camp

This camp near Brigg was designated as Camp 81. Until fairly recently, this German working camp remained in a semi-derelict condition. It was demolished to make way for housing. Originally Italian prisoners of war were housed here, and then subsequently Germans. It had a capacity of around 750 prisoners. There was a larger water tower and a number of prefabricated huts, which Italian prisoners built between 1942 and 1943. Some of the rooms and huts still retained furniture and prisoners' belongings, along with artwork on the walls.

### The Rectory Camp

Located at Bassingham, it was designated as Camp 138. This was used as a hostel for German prisoners of war. The original building is now believed to be a nursing home.

### Castlethorpe Camp

This was Camp 148 and was also situated near Brigg. This German working camp had nearly 40 huts and it lay between Castlethorpe Hall and Castlethorpe Covert.

### Fulney Park

Based at Low Fulney, near Spalding, it was known as Camp 153. This was a relatively large German working camp.

### Heath Camp

This was at the Pottergate Plantation, Wellingore and was designated as Camp 156. It was formerly RAF Wellingore which opened in 1917. It was reopened as an airfield in 1935 and expanded up to 1940. The airfield closed in 1945. The site was used as a prisoner of war camp for both German and Ukrainian prisoners of war but it was returned to farmland in the early 1950s.

One of the notable personalities that lived nearby and operated from RAF Wellingore was Wing Commander Guy Gibson. He was based there with RAF 29 Squadron when he shot down his very first German aircraft off the coast of Skegness in March 1941.

### Weelsby Camp

Based near Grimsby, it had the designation of Camp 170. This camp was also given the number of Camp 292. The Weelsby woods area was used as a camp for Italian prisoners of war in hutted camps. In fact, two of the small buildings operated as a café and toilet until as late as 2006 when they were pulled down. Some foundations can still be seen around the area. The camp was a large one, with nine watchtowers and a perimeter fence.

### Willingham House

Camp 256 was at Willingham House in Market Rasen. The house survived for just less than 200 years, having been built in 1790 and demolished in 1967. During the First World War, it was used as a convalescent home and it is listed as a German working camp in the Second World War. There were several attempted escapes. The Germans were later replaced by Italian prisoners of war. After the war, the house was used as a civil defence training centre. The Royal Engineers blew up the main building, which had become structurally unsound. They carried out the demolition to avoid damaging Home Office buildings on the site.

### Kirmington Camp
This was near Caistor and was designated Camp 292A. This is now the site of Humberside airport and formerly RAF Kirmington. The camp consisted of a number of concrete huts, although some of the remaining buildings were probably originally RAF buildings and may have been used as part of the prisoner of war camp. Many of the buildings were pulled down around 2008.

### Donna Nook Airfield
Another Lincolnshire prisoner of war camp was Donna Nook Airfield, which was also numbered Camp 292 or 292B. This was also on the site of a former RAF airfield, called Donna Nook. The site is believed to have been on Ark Road, North Somercotes. It closed as an RAF airfield in 1945 but became a NATO bombing range and is still in use.

### Usselby Camp
Camp 407 was at Usselby Camp in Usselby, near Market Rasen. This was a large base camp and it was used to house German officers. Usselby is also the site of a deserted medieval village.

### Canwick Camp
Based in Canwick, near Lincoln, it was given the number of Camp 1012. There are references to elements of the Royal Army Service Corps being at Canwick Camp from early December 1944, which confirms the fact that it was an existing camp consisting of a number of Nissen huts. At some point it was put to use as a German working camp and the Nissen huts were located around a playing field.

Potterhanworth Booths prisoner of war camp, a relic of WW2 that once housed German and Italian POWs. [*Image courtesy of Richard Croft, http://www.geograph.org.uk.*]

### Potterhanworth Booths

It housed Italian prisoners of war initially, then German ones. Potterhanworth Booths is a tiny hamlet close to Potterhanworth itself. The prisoners of war worked on the local estate and in farms in the area.

### London

### 22 Hyde Park Gardens

This was designated Camp 17 and was the home of the London District Cage. Essentially it was a large mansion building surrounded by barbed wire and with armed guards. It was used to interrogate suspected war criminals. The Cage was commanded by the Chief of the War Crimes Investigation Unit, Colonel Scotland.

## Carpenter's Road Camp
This was situated in Stratford, London and was designated Camp 30. This prisoner of war camp was built on the site of a group of factories that had been bombed. Initially the camp was for Italian prisoners, who would have worn dark battledress displaying a large, yellow circle or diamond on the back. Later, the camp became a German prisoner of war working camp.

## Scrubs Lane Camp
This was based close to Wormwood Scrubs prison in Shepherd's Bush and was designated Camp 32. The Scrubs Lane Camp was a standard German working camp but, during the Second World War, part of Wormwood Scrubs prison was being used by MI5 and the War Department. By the end of hostilities, a section of the hospital wing at Wormwood Scrubs was being used as condemned quarters for prisoners from Wandsworth and Pentonville prisons.

## Newlands House
Set on Tooting Bec Road, it was designated as Camp 125 and was originally an asylum. It was used during the Second World War as a German working camp.

## Becton Marshes Camp
It was given the number Camp 183. The marshes have now almost completely disappeared and have been covered with housing and new developments. Becton was originally part of East Ham and for many years it was used as allotments, but there was certainly a large prisoner of war camp there, of which there is no visible sign remaining. The camp was close to West Ham football stadium and housed large groups of Italian prisoners of war and also Germans.

## Hampton Park
Hampton Park was Camp 193. After being shipped to England, the prisoners were transported by railway wagons and then lorries into Hampton Park. The camp appears to have been tented, and German-speaking Polish officers screened the prisoners on arrival.

German officers at Trent Park Camp in 1943. [*Image courtesy of the German Federal Archive.*]

Prisoners included a German who was captured in Holland in January, 1945.

### Shooters Hill

Camp 1020 was Shooters Hill, Woodlands Farm in Woolwich. This area was the site of many anti-aircraft guns during the Second World War. It was also the site of a German working camp and housed 1,000 German and Italian prisoners. There were huge changes in the geography of this area between 1936 and 1944. The prisoner of war camp was on part of the golf course with the cookhouse located on the 17th green. The much-bombed area returned to a full-sized golf course after the war, although nine holes continued to be played despite the presence of both the anti-aircraft battery and the prisoner of war camp.

## Middlesex

### Cockfosters and Trent Park Camps
There is some confusion regarding two camps, 10 and 11A. Both were in Barnet and one was known as Cockfosters Camp and the other Trent Park Camp. The latter consisted of a single, large building with barbed wire, watchtowers and pillboxes.

### Rayner's Lane
There was another camp designated 11A at Rayner's Lane in Harrow-on-the-Hill.

### Oxhey Lane and The Ministry of Works Camps
This was designated as Camp 122 and was situated on Uxbridge Road, Hatch End. This was the site of a German working camp. A sports centre now occupies the site. The Ministry of Works Camp was also thought to be on the same site and was designated Camp 274.

German officers posed for a photograph at Trent Park Camp in November, 1943. [*Image courtesy of the German Federal Archive.*]

### Osterley Park Camp
Osterley Park Camp, Wyke Green, Isleworth was designated Camp 562, but it was also given the number 681. Osterley Park is now in the western suburbs of London and the original manor house was built there in the 1570s. The grounds were used to train the first members of the Home Guard, training ceased there in 1941. The site opened as a prisoner of war camp in 1943, initially with Italian prisoners. Many of these prisoners worked at the nearby Crown Cork Plant. There were 19 huts and a dining room.

### West Ridge Camp
This was situated in Greenford and given the number of Camp 669. There was a reference to the site in the Houses of Parliament in December 1946, which suggests that the status of the prisoner of war camp was already under review. In fact, many of the huts there were being used as offices for clerks who worked for the record office connected to the occupation of Germany. The West Ridge Camp, according to a House of Commons statement, was still occupied by prisoners of war, although half of it had been handed over for use as temporary housing for those that had lost their homes during the bombing.

### Capel House Camp
Located in Bullsmoor Lane, Enfield, it was designated Camp 1003. Capel House is now known as Capel Manor and the house and Seventeenth Century walled garden are open to the public. It was used at the end of the war as a German working camp. The main building is Eighteenth Century and was remodelled at the beginning of the Twentieth Century.

### Norfolk

### Hempton Green Camp
Based near Fakenham, it was designated Camp 82 and is now a caravan park. Originally, the camp housed Italian prisoners of war and then became a German working camp.

## Uplands Camp

Situated in Diss, it was known as Camp 131 and housed Italian prisoners of war, until around 1946.

## Kimberley Park

Kimberley Park, Kimberley was Camp 132. The camp was probably located in and around Kimberley Hall whose grounds were originally designed by Capability Brown in 1762. The main house was built in 1712 and the camp's huts were located under the trees, by the driveway to the house.

## Mousehold Heath Camp

This was designated as Camp 253, on the outskirts of the city of Norwich. Mousehold Heath was an airfield and it became a civilian aerodrome after the Second World War. Although it is listed as a German working camp, we do know that the site also was used to hold Ukrainian prisoners of war. Incidentally, a V2 rocket also landed on the site.

## Sutton Bridge

Sutton Bridge, Holbeach was the site for Camp 254. This was a former RAF airfield that had opened in the 1920s and was developed in the late 1930s. It was inactive as an airfield from 1946 and was a German working camp. A power station and an agricultural station are now situated in the area.

## Snettisham Scalp

This was designated as Camp 255 and was literally on the shoreline. For many years, it was used as a gunnery range. Italian, German and Ukrainian prisoners of war were housed here. There were a number of Nissen huts, and after the prisoners of war left the site became a centre that housed European volunteers. It is now the site of a chemical works.

## Deopham Green

Deopham Green in Attleborough, was the site of Camps 271 and 272. It was a former RAF airfield that had been built in 1942 and opened for use by the US Air Force in January 1944. It was formally handed back to the RAF in October 1945 and had been listed as a German working camp.

### North Lynn Farm Camp
Now the site of a chemical works, it was previously designated as Camp 280 and held up to 5,000 prisoners of war. In 1947, it had a large influx of additional prisoners of war, as another local prisoner of war camp had been flooded.

### Wolterton Camp
Wolterton Hall is a Georgian house in Aylsham and was built in the 1720s. It was designated Camp 409. The prisoner of war camp is believed to have been located along the drive and in woods in the grounds. It was used as a base camp.

### Kilverstone Hall
Located near Thetford in the grounds of a Seventeenth Century house that was rebuilt in 1913, it had the designation of Camp 630.

## Northamptonshire

### Hill Farm Estate
Camp 98 was a German working camp based at Hill Farm Estate, Little Addington. There are some remains still here of this former Italian and then German camp that had a capacity of around 550 prisoners.

### Boughton Park Camp
Based in Northampton, it was designated Camp 35 and 259 and was also known as Boughton Park Camp, Boughton Camp, Weekley Camp and Boughton Hall Camp. However, it appears it became a standard German camp that was based in a heavily wooded area. The camp inmates produced their own magazine or newsletter entitled *Lagerzeitung*.

This was something that a number of German prisoners of war did, including those incarcerated in Harperley Camp, County

Former Ordnance depot and Second World War POW (Prisoner of War) camp, Boughton. [*Image courtesy of Steve Fareham http://www.geograph.org.uk.*]

Durham, who had their own magazine entitled *Der Quell Lagerzeitung Camp 95*.

### Byfield Camp
Located along the Boddington Road, near Daventry, it was designated Camp 87. The camp was initially used to house Italian prisoners of war and several of the original buildings still survive.

### Park Farm
Located at Thorny, near Peterborough, the German working camp was designated as Camp 265. Aerial photography reveals traces of tracks and some building foundations.

## King's Cliffe

Camp 702 was King's Cliffe, near Peterborough. Although the location of the camp is often quoted as being within the village, it was actually on the site of RAF King's Cliffe. A holiday camp was built there in 1922 and the RAF airfield in 1943.

## Weedon Camp

Near Weedon Beck, it was given the designation Camp 1010. It appears that the camp here was located in West Street and originally there were Italian prisoners of war. A number of children had been evacuated from the London area to Weedon prior to this. The Italians were replaced with Germans, around 1944, and this was used as a working camp.

# Northumberland

## Featherstone Park Camp

Located near Haltwhistle, it was designated Camp 18. This was a large base camp with two prisoner compounds and many huts. It was originally built in 1944 to house US troops earmarked for the liberation of France in 1944. Once the Americans had been deployed, Italian prisoners of war were moved in but, in 1945, they were all moved out and it became a high security unit for so-called Black Nazis. These were men who were believed to be dangerous and would only be repatriated once they had been denazified. They included U-boat crewmen, German civil servants and other members of the German armed forces. At its peak, there were some 4,000 officers and around 600 orderlies and by that stage upwards of 200 huts with around 25,000 Germans held over a three-year period. In 1947 the barbed wire fencing was removed and many of the men were allowed to work on local farms. The camp was extremely well-organised, with a theatre, a library, and chapel as well as other facilities for the prisoners. Captain Sulzbach was the camp interpreter from 1946 and played a vital role at the camp in the rehabilitation of prisoners. He even founded the Featherstone Park Group to foster Anglo-German friendships. Although the buildings are

Nicknamed 'Death Valley' because of its isolated location by the American troops who used the camp as a training ground, it later held both Italian prisoners of war and Germans. [*Image courtesy of Les Hull http://www.geograph. org.uk.*]

now gone, it is still possible to see the layout and scope of the camp.

### *Darras Hill Camp*
Based in Ponteland, it was designated Camp 69. Although this is listed as a German working camp, a Red Cross visit in May of 1944 noted that there were 760 Italian prisoners there. They had arrived at the beginning of 1943 and tended to work on local farms. The regime at the camp slackened after September 1943 when the Italians dropped out of the Axis. The vast majority of the Italians had left by the end of 1944, but some remained, working on local farms or as labourers and they were certainly housed outside the camp itself. It is believed that the first Germans began arriving via Newcastle by bus in March 1945. When the camp was re-inspected

by the Red Cross in late May, there were some 830 Germans in the camp. The prison population steadily increased, with a number of the men being transferred from camps in the United States and, nearly 11 months later, there were over 1,300. The vast majority of prisoners were being housed in the camp itself, along with others who were in hostels. A year later there were 1,200 men but by October 1947 the figure had dropped to 1,000 men.

It is believed that the last German prisoners of war left the camp towards the end of 1948 and refugees were being housed there, working on local farms and for other local businesses. The refugees appear to have remained there for at least a year. In 1950 the old prison camp was largely demolished and in the early spring of the following year the camp became a civil defence training camp. This was finally demolished a decade later. At its height there were 19 prisoner of war huts and there were four watchtowers, but these were dismantled at some point in 1945.

### Wooler and Hetton House Camps
Camp number 105 was called Wooler Camp on Brewery Road, Wooler. There was also a second camp, Hetton House Camp, at Chatton Wooler that had been allocated the same camp number. Both camps appear to have been German working camps and both sites can still be seen.

### Kitty Brewster Farm
Camp 291 was at Kitty Brewster Farm in Blythe. It is likely that the camp is under one of the trading estates now situated here. It was originally an anti-aircraft battery site that is listed as being a German working camp.

### Lord Mayor's Camp
Lord Mayor's Camp near Amble was designated as Camp 635. Amble was a former holiday camp and it was used until 1938, having been established four years earlier. There were a number of huts that were originally named after stately homes. Guard towers and barbed wire were put up around the area and it became a prisoner of war camp. The site is now a caravan park.

### Byreness Camp

This was designated Camp 667 and was near Redesdale. This particular part of Northumberland has a long tradition of association with the army and the nearby Otterburn army training estate was established in 1911.

### Tyne J Camp

This was given the designated number of Camp 699 and was at South Gosforth, near the greyhound stadium. This was originally a barrage balloon station.

## Nottinghamshire

### Serlby Hall Camp

This Eighteenth Century mansion at Serlby was Camp 143. During the First World War it had been used as an auxiliary military hospital and became a prisoner of war camp during the Second World War.

### Carlton Hall

Carlton Hall near Worksop was also designated as Camp 143. It held Italian and German prisoners of war towards the end of the war, after a British tank regiment that had previously been based there had moved out.

### Wollaton Hall Park Camp

This was designated as Camp 166. Wollaton Hall is an Elizabethan manor and deer park set in 500 acres. There was a huge tented city that housed members of the US 82nd Airborne Division. They arrived in the area in March 1944. Excavations in 2009 discovered the camp's fence line and the fact that several of the buildings had been built using local brick. There were large numbers of buildings all across the parkland and many of the foundations survive below the ground. The camp at its height housed around 4,000 prisoners and the majority of the buildings appear to have been demolished in the early 1950s.

The last of the prisoner of war camp huts at Wollaton Hall Park Camp. The northern part of the park housed huts for the German prisoners of war between 1945-48. Most were removed, with four left standing for years and used as school changing rooms. This is the last one standing. [*Image courtesy of John Sutton http://www.geograph.org.uk.*]

### Tollerton Hall Camp
Located in Tollerton, this was designed both Camp 169 and Camp 613. US troops were at Tollerton Hall until the end of May 1944 and the existing army camp was subsequently converted into a prisoner of war camp. It would also appear that the majority of the camp was covered in tents, with very few permanent buildings. Consequently, very little evidence remains of the camp today.

### Norton Camp
Based at Cuckney near Edwinstowe and Mansfield, it was designated as Camp 174. As well as housing German prisoners of war, the base camp was used to house former Tsarist Russian

soldiers. These men were stateless. The official closing ceremony of the Norton Camp YMCA School for prisoners of war took place on 16th April, 1948. At that stage, there were some 439 prisoners still in the camp. There was a large open-air theatre that had been built amongst the trees, which had been constructed in 1944 by German officers.

### Carburton Camp
It was near Worksop and was designated Camp 181 and Camp 249. In May 1944, this was designated as an overflow camp. By 31st March, 1945, 1,634 prisoners were moved out of the Island Farm Camp (Camp 198) to Carburton as a result of the escape attempt from Camp 198. The Carburton Camp was a large complex of huts with watchtowers and double wire fencing.

### RAF Camp Langar
This was designated as Camp 262. It was built as an airfield in early 1942, with a number of Nissen huts and other buildings. Originally both the RAF and the US Air Force used the camp; the latter used it as a troop carrier base. Lancaster bombers certainly stayed on the airfield until March 1945. It was then used for a short period of time for German prisoners of war and then for displaced persons (i.e. stateless people such as the Tsarist soldiers). The Royal Canadian Air Force took it over temporarily in 1952 and actually ended up using it for 11 years.

### Boughton Camp
Located at New Ollerton, it was designated as Camp 633 and Camp 656. New Ollerton was set up as a model village in the 1920s. The site of the camp was formerly the home of the US Army 1961st Engineer Depot Company. Some of the German prisoners of war held there had made the long trip to Boughton via Canada. Many of the German prisoners of war had returned home by 1948. The camp, which is now Boughton Industrial Estate North, once also housed Italian prisoners of war.

The Nissen huts of Boughton prisoner of war camp now form part of Boughton Industrial Estate North. [*Image courtesy of Steve Fareham.*]

## Oxfordshire

### Old Windmills Camp

This was situated on Blackthorne Hill near Bicester and designated as Camp 33, Camp 632 and Camp 653. The mainly Italian prisoners of war worked on local farms or cleared ditches and maintained fencing. Some also worked in the local clay pits. The camp was disposed of in 1963.

### Harcourt Hill Camp

This was in North Hinksey, a village two miles to the west of Oxford and it became Camp 43. Little evidence remains of the former German working camp site, which was situated at the top of the hill.

### North Camp

Located at Nettlebed, Henley on Thames, it was designated as Camp 246 and was a large camp built for upwards of 2,000 men. US Engineers were stationed here from 1942. The camp was used as a German working camp before being turned over to European refugees. The camp was demolished in the late 1940s.

### Graven Hill

Camp 553 was at Graven Hill, Bicester and was also designated as Camp 683. There were, in fact, four complexes of buildings on Graven Hill, which were put up by the US Army. It is listed as a German working camp and could have included Camp 657, Camp 1011 and Camp D30.

### No 9 Tented Camp

No 9 Tented Camp, in Arncott near Bicester was designated as Camp 657 and was a German working camp.

### Shed D35, Graven Hill

Also designated as Camp 657 was Shed D35 on Graven Hill, Arncott. It is believed that this was originally an ordnance depot. Camp 1011's location is also listed as Graven Hill, where it was also known as Camp D30.

### Eynsham Park

Camp 661A was located at Eynsham Park, either in the grounds of Eynsham Hall or close to a sawmill in the area.

### Shotover House

This was designated Camp 687. The house was built in the early Eighteenth Century. There was a German working camp based in the grounds. Very little remains of this site as it has been returned to parkland and some of it was destroyed when a road was widened.

### Horgard Barracks

Based at Shrivenham, it was Camp 695. This was a German working camp, which seems to have been a tented camp with a basic compound and watchtowers. The original site is now covered with housing and vehicle parking.

## Shropshire

### St Martin's Camp

St Martin's Camp, or Camp 100, in St Martin's, near Oswestry is now an industrial estate but it was first used to house Italians and then Germans. Several of the buildings still exist, although they have subsequently been converted to civilian use.

### Mile House

Set on Shrewsbury Road, Oswestry, it was designated Camp 8. This building still exists and was used during the Second World War as a base camp.

### Prees Heath

Prees Heath, Whitchurch was the site of Camp 16. The site had already been an important training camp and hospital during the First World War. It was also used as a dispersal point when troops were demobilised at the end of that war. In 1939, it became a screening camp for German and Austrian refugees, where they were interned in a large, tented village, which was able to house up to 2,000. It temporarily became a prisoner of war camp, but only remained in operation until the beginning of October 1941. At that point, it was converted into RAF Tilstock when three concrete runways were built.

### Green Fields Camp

This was located on Ellesmere Road in Shrewsbury and designated Camp 23.

### Acksea Camp

This was in Kinnerley, Oswestry and designated as Camp 34. It initially housed Italian prisoners but, ultimately, became a German working camp. In 1941, the War Department requisitioned a railway line from Shrewsbury to Llanymynech, which straddled the border with England and Wales. It is believed that up to 600 Italian prisoners worked on constructing this railway line. The War Department also established a vast ammunition storage dump at a secret depot in Kinnerley, containing some 200 huge storage sheds. These sheds were camouflaged with turfed roofs, and were built around the village of Kinnerley. Eventually, each shed was served by a railway siding. The military continued to use the railway line until it was closed in 1960. The area remains a military training area.

### Sheriffhales Camp

This camp at Shifnal, in the east of the county, was designated as Camp 71. The camp, which was initially occupied by Italian prisoners of war, was situated on land belonging to a manor. After the Italian surrender in 1943 Sheriffhales camp became a standard type German working camp. The prisoners worked with local farmers. After the armistice, the former prisoner of war camp housed displaced refugees from former Eastern European countries.

### Sheet Camp

This was designated as Camp 84 and was near Ludlow. This was another German working camp but only the original water tower remains to mark the site.

### Adderley Hall

Located in Adderley near Market Drayton, this was designated as Camp 192. It had been used as a reinforcement camp because of fears that the Germans may invade Britain. Later on during the war, it was the home of US personnel. The hall was used as a base camp for prisoners, but was demolished during the 1950s.

### Hawkstone Park

Hawkstone Park at Weston was known as Camp 240 and also as Camp 285. Now reverted to its former hotel and golf course, the park is a Grade I historic park. During the Second World War, a part of the extensive grounds were used as a German working camp.

### Davenport House

Set in Worfield, Bridgnorth, this was given the allocation of both Camp 272 and Camp 272A. Davenport House is a Grade I listed

Georgian mansion house. The prisoner of war camp was a standard German working camp.

### Wilcott Camp
Wilcott Camp, Nesscliffe was designated as Camp 591. Formerly a Central Ammunition Depot, many of the pre-existing buildings were used to house the prisoners of war. Later, the camp was used by displaced European persons. The site is currently used as a military training area and covers around 1,681 acres.

### South Camp, North Camp and E Camp
A camp of many parts: this camp at Donnington, near Wellington, had three designations – South Camp was designated 651, Camp 659 (also known as North Camp) and also Camp 1004 (also known as E Camp). It was originally used as an ordnance depot before being converted into a prisoner of war camp.

### 83 Ordnance Supply Depot
This camp on Soulton Road in Wem was known as Camp 679. It may well have been a subsidiary camp to Hawkstone Camp (Camp 240 and Camp 285). Camp 679 was also the home of Quartermaster Unit and hospital personnel.

### Somerset

### Ashton Court
Located at Bower Ashton, it had the prison camp designated number of 6A. This is now a mansion and country park that is open to the general public. There are very little remains today of this prisoner of war camp.

### Colley Lane Camp
Based at Bridgwater, it was designated as Camp 37. The camp had capacity for around 500 German prisoners of war. This camp was linked to Goathurst Camp, which was also in Bridgwater.

### Goathurst Camp

Located at Goathurst, Bridgwater, it was designated Camp 44 and housed approximately 500 Italians in huts. These men were employed in farming and given a degree of freedom, although their brown battledress uniform displayed large yellow patches to indicate their prisoner status.

### Penleigh Camp

At Wookey Hole, near Wells, was Camp 107. The Penleigh Camp, on Wookey Hole Road, was a German working camp comprising of men that had been captured in Normandy. The prisoner of war camp consisted of a number of single storey huts. It is understood that the site is now covered with housing. Some of the former Camp 107 is covered with the Penleigh Works. *See Stoberry Park Camp.*

### Brockley Camp

Based near Brockley, close to where Bristol International Airport is now located, it was known as Camp 403. There was a small prisoner of war camp here, with a maximum capacity of around 300, which typically housed Italian prisoners of war and, later, German prisoners. To the west of Brockley is a huge Iron Age hill fort.

### Barwick House Camp

Located at Barwick, near Yeovil, it was designated as Camp 405. The house was built in 1770 and the prisoner of war camp on the estate initially housed Italian prisoners of war and, later, German prisoners from Normandy. It was used as a base camp. Very little now remains of the camp as it has been returned to parkland.

### Cross Keys Camp

Based at Norton Fitzwarren, near Taunton, it had the designation of Camp 665. This was another relatively small prisoner of war camp which, again, held around 300 prisoners of war. It is close to the home of 40 Commando of the Royal Marines, based at Norton Manor Camp. The site is now mainly comprised of the Langford Mead business park.

Second World War supply depot at Norton Fitzwarren, one of the remaining parts of the prisoner of war camp at the army complex. [*Image courtesy of Martin Bodman http://www.geograph.co.uk.*]

### Stoberry Park Camp

This was at Stoberry in Wells and was designated Camp 666. This camp was built by US troops in 1943. Originally around 750 American troops were stationed here. Stoberry Camp initially held Italian prisoners of war and then from 1945, German prisoners. As the camp filled up, the prisoners were sent to Maesbury Camp and we also know that, by early 1947, the Germans had been transferred to Penleigh Camp. The 20+ remaining huts were turned over to civilian use, but it was not until January 1948 that the barbed wire was removed. The huts continued to stand on the site until the 1950s and, after that, they were demolished and houses were built on the site.

### Houndstone Camp

Based near Yeovil, Houndstone Camp was a large army camp. We know that several buildings in the camp were destroyed by incendiary bombs in October 1940. In 1942, the site was occupied

The stained glass window at St Mary the Virgin in East Chinnock was created after the war by a German Master Glazier and former prisoner of war, Gunther Anton, in gratitude to the locals for how he was treated as a prisoner. He worked on a farm during the war, after being shot down over Southampton whilst serving in the German Luftwaffe, and attended the church. The windows took him 26 years to complete and he died shortly after seeing them dedicated in 1989. [*Image courtesy of Sarah Smith http://www.geograph.org.uk.*]

by African-American troops. American soldiers remained there until at least the D-Day landings in 1944. The camp became a prisoner of war camp towards the latter part of the war. The site itself is now an industrial estate, although a couple of the original buildings still remain.

## Staffordshire

### Flaxley Green Camp
This was designated as both Camp 16 and 175. It was a large camp that comprised six compounds; three with permanent huts and the other three tented. The site was also located on Stile Cop field.

### Wolseley Road Camp
Based in Rugeley, it was used as a German working camp and was designated Camp 96. References to this camp may well refer to one that was on Stile Cop, which is now a popular area for cycling.

### Shugborough Park Hospital
Camp 99 was at Shugborough Park Hospital, at Great Haywood. It had a bed capacity of around 500 men. It was built during 1943 to be used by the US Army, originally as a 1,000-bed hospital. It was subsequently taken over as a prisoner of war camp. There is very little evidence left, as much of the ground has now been returned to its original condition as parkland.

### Loxley Hall Camp
Based in Loxley, near Uttoxeter, it was allocated the number Camp 134. The hall was built in the early-Nineteenth Century and the substantial mansion is now a school. The camp here was used for displaced persons in the late 1940s and there are references to Latvians still being on site in 1948.

### Pendeford Hall Camp
Located at Codsal, near Wolverhampton, it was Camp 151. Pendeford Hall was built in the Seventeenth Century and was requisitioned during the Second World War and was used as a German working camp. It was partly demolished in 1953, with the final demolition taking place in the late 1960s. The site now houses a caravan park.

### Lawn Camp and Halfpenny Green
Camp 151A was on Coven Lane. This was a former anti-aircraft battery site and operated as an annexe to the Pendeford Hall site (Camp 151). Also attached to this was Camp 151B on Halfpenny Green. This site had originally been an RAF airfield. It is now the site of Wolverhampton Airport and Aviation Park. The airfield was originally built in 1939 and there are several Second World War vintage buildings on the site, some of which may well have been used as part of the camp.

### Teddesley Hall Camp

Based in Penkridge, it was known as Camp 194. Penkridge is most closely associated with an attempt to launch a mass breakout by German prisoners in December 1944. Some 13 German prisoners got away and, although reports differ, six were caught in Derby, two in Walsall, two in Wolverhampton, and two in Liverpool. Another report suggests that four were caught in Leicestershire. One of the men probably escaped or went to ground. There was also a second attempt on Easter Sunday 1945, this time using a tunnel, but this was discovered. Attached to this site was a second camp in Penkridge, designated Camp 194 and called Council Houses Camp because of its location.

### Stretton Hall Camp

This was designated Camp 564. The hall was built in the Eighteenth Century and the prisoner of war camp was located near Hall Farm.

## Suffolk

### Botesdale

Camp 56 was situated on Bury Road in Botesdale, near Diss. This was a standard type working camp that has subsequently been demolished. All that remains as evidence of the original prisoner of war camp is a large section of the water tower. According to the *Suffolk and Essex Free Press* dated 27th May, 1948:

> There were heartbreaking scenes at Bury [St Edmunds] railway station when a large number of German prisoners from Fordham and Botesdale started on their way home after two and a half years in this country. The party included some seventy high ranking naval and army officers.

### Victoria Camp

Situated at Mildenhall, it had the designated number of Camp 85. It was a purpose-built German working camp at Codson Hill, but the first prisoners were Italian, and it is probable that they may well have been involved in its construction. The camp remained open until around 1948.

### Redgrave Park Hospital

Located near Diss, it was designated as Camp 231. Formerly Redgrave Park Hall, it had become the largest US Air Force hospital in the country. The hospital had been built to serve the US 8th Air Force. The prisoner of war camp was built on the Warren. Some of the footings of the original buildings still remain.

### Ellough Airfield

The airfield near Beccles was designated as Camp 258. Ellough was built in 1943 for use by the USAAF, and the RAF then also used the site. It would appear that the airfield was used for a time as a German working camp. The disused airfield is now the site of a Sunday market.

### Hardwick Heath Camp

Camp 260 was near Bury St Edmunds. Built initially to house Italian prisoners, this camp contained approximately 64 huts. Later, it became a standard type German working camp. The prisoners worked on local farms and on road constructions. It is believed that the Mildenhall Road was built with the assistance of some Italian prisoners.

### Flixton Airfield

Based at Flixton, near Bungay, it was designated as Camp 273. This was formerly RAF Bungay and, from November 1943 to April 1945, it was home to part of the US Air Force. It operated as a German working camp for a short period of time. The camp's administrative headquarters would have been on the current site, which is now an aviation museum. A Bungay base camp is also listed as Camp 171, which was also located on or near the airfield.

### Debach Airfield

This site near Woodbridge had the designation of Camp 273 and Camp 273A. Confusingly, former RAF Debach was given the same designation as Flixton. It, too, had been home to the USAAF's 8th

Air Force from April 1944 to around August 1945. For a time, the airfield became a German working camp and then a centre for refugees. It was closed around 1948. Most of the site is now part of a couple of farms. There are plans to restore the control tower for use as a museum.

## Surrey

### Kempton Park Camp
Camp 9 was used as a reception centre. It used many of the racecourse buildings and large numbers of tents were also put up. There was a perimeter fence and guard towers.

### Kingwood Camp
Located at Wormley, this was designated Camp 23.

### Merrow Down Camp
This site near Guildford was known as Camp 57. Initially, the camp had the capacity to house more than 800 Italian prisoners captured in North Africa. The camp was made up of a number of huts, each of which could sleep a maximum of 40 men. Each corner of the camp had an outlook tower. The Italian prisoners would work with local farmers and carry out road construction and maintenance. After the armistice, German prisoners also occupied the prison camp and some of the satellite hostels that were attached to it, with some prisoners remaining there until 1948. Merrow Down Camp was the regional headquarters for a total of 14 prisoner of war camps and their satellites. The camp was demolished in the 1950s but there are now notices on the downland by Guildford Golf Club giving information about the camp and also its impact on the environment, including the small blue butterfly.

### Ruskin Avenue
Based in Kew, it was designated as Camp 144. It is interesting to note that this is the site of the National Archives. The Post Office stores, situated on Occupation Road, were used to house Italian prisoners of war during the Second World War.

### Westonacres Camp

This was in Woodmansterne, near Banstead. Designated as Camp 239, there were nearly 600 Italians at this camp as late as October 1945. In April 1946, it was transformed into a German working camp and, in early May, the Italians were repatriated, with upwards of 1,500 Germans being brought to the camp. At one point, the headquarters were located in a golf club house on Shirley Church Road. This camp used a number of hostels in Banstead, Chessington, Staines, Croydon and Whitten, amongst others. There were still over 860 prisoners of war in February 1948 but this had dropped to 475 in March, and the camp was finally disbanded in the middle of May 1948. The Germans were involved in the construction of government offices and other building projects.

### Topsite

Camp 275 was Topsite, a German working camp at Thames Ditton.

### Barnhouse Farm

This site at Shipley, near Horsham, was Camp 658. An advanced landing ground was built on this site, which was, in effect, a temporary airfield. After the Normandy landings, its usage was changed to a prisoner of war camp, housing mainly German prisoners.

### Old Dean Common Camp

This was given the designations of Camp 674 and Camp 675. There are also references to the camp being designated Camp 1016. Located near Camberley, the Old Dean Common was used to train Free French forces during the Second World War. It was a significant existing camp before it was transferred for usage as a German working camp towards the end of the war. The whole area must have been cleared by the early 1950s, because a large housing estate began to spring up on the common. Some locals remember living in Nissen huts in the 1950s and that, until the mid-1960s, there was still a water tower in evidence.

### Raynes Park Camp

Situated on Bushey Road, it was given the designation of Camp 1026, the final number in the designation listings. Raynes Park is actually now a suburb of the London Borough of Merton and is close to Wimbledon. By 1948, the German working camp had been abandoned, and bombed-out local residents were living in the camp whilst new council homes were being constructed. It was the site of anti-aircraft guns earlier in the war.

### Sussex

### Kingsfold Camp

This was situated on Kingsfold Close off Marringdean Road, Billingshurst and was designated Camp 46. It was a standard-type German working camp.

### Normanhurst Camp

Normanhurst Camp near Battle was Camp 145. This large manor house was built in the late-Nineteenth Century. It was used during the First World War as a military hospital and the house and grounds were used as a German working camp during the Second World War. The house was demolished in 1951 and is now a caravan site.

### Brook House

Located in Hammingden Lane, Ardingley, it was designated as Camp 238 and was a German working camp. The house itself was once a substantial family home, but it is now split into a number of individual residences.

### Seafield School

This site at Cooden Down, near Bexhill, was Camp 631. The Cooden Down area was also used during the First World War. Originally, it had tents and, later, more solid wooden buildings. It was used as a training camp during the First World War, for example, by members of the Royal Sussex Regiment. It was, therefore, an existing army camp which enabled its use as a prisoner of war camp towards the end of the Second World War.

## No 2 Camp

Situated at Sheffield Park, Uckfield, it was designated as Camp 1017. The National Trust now own Sheffield Park Garden. The Sheffield Park Estate is mentioned in the Domesday Book and it was requisitioned during the Second World War, with the house and gardens becoming the headquarters for a Canadian armoured division. It was at this stage that a number of Nissen huts were erected around the gardens and in the woods. This made it ideal for a German working camp later in the war.

## Warwickshire

### Long Marston Camp

This was designated Camp 6 and had been an ordnance depot during the war. It was not a large prisoner of war camp and, in the post-war years, it was reassigned as a Polish resettlement camp.

### Cloister Croft

This site near Leamington Spa was Camp 25.

### Ettington Park Camp

Located near Stratford-upon-Avon, it was originally an Italian but later a German working camp. The camp had been designated Camp 31. It was housed at Ettington Hall, a neo-Gothic mansion house in the Stour Valley. The hall had become a nursing home by 1935 but was converted into a prisoner of war camp. By 1943, the camp had a capacity of 800 men.

### Castle Camp

The camp at Maxstoke, Coleshill was eventually to become a German working camp and had been designated as Camp 39. In 1940 Maxstoke Castle had been used for the storage of aircraft engine components in order to protect them from bomb damage. At the same time the prisoner of war camp for Italian prisoners was established in the grounds, which are now part of a golf course.

### Birdingbury Camp
Situated near Bourton on Dunsmore, it was a German working camp and is thought to have had a capacity of 500 prisoners of war. There is very little left of this camp, which was designated Camp 97.

### Racecourse Camp
Based a Warwick Racecourse, it was designated as Camp 140. The racecourse was first built in 1808 and is still a leading horseracing course. It was converted to a fairly large camp, which housed German and Italian prisoners of war.

### Merevale Hall Camp
Located in Atherstone, it was designated as Camp 195. Merevale Hall was a US Army camp. The original building was rebuilt in the 1840s. The camp here is also listed as Camp 241 and it was both a base camp and a German working camp.

### Arbury Hall
Near Nuneaton, it was designated as Camp 196. The hall was built on the ruins of a Twelfth Century priory, surrounded by parkland. This was used as a base camp during the war and it is not thought that there are any remains of the camp, as the grounds have subsequently been returned to parkland. German prisoners of war rebuilt the church at Chilvers Coton, and a German artisan, who was also held as a prisoner, sculpted one of the crosses in the church.

### Stratford-upon-Avon Camp
This was designated as Camp 232 and there were a number of army camps in the area.

### Marlborough Farm Camp
Based near Kineton, it was known as Camp 579. The Ministry of Defence is still at the former Marlborough barracks, which may

have been the centre or at least the administrative headquarters of this prisoner of war camp.

Marlborough barracks is located virtually on the site of the English Civil War battlefield of Edgehill. This was the first major battle of the first civil war and fought on 23rd October, 1642.

### Stoneleigh Camp

Stoneleigh, near Coventry, was Camp 667 and Camp 667A. This was a training camp and a US military hospital. It was also the location of a German working camp towards the end of the Second World War. It is now home to an annual militaria show.

### Number 3 Camp

ESCD, Long Marston was designated as Camp 685. This is listed as a German working camp, but Italian prisoners of war were there before this. Afterwards, there were displaced Polish people at the site. An Italian prisoner of war apparently got himself involved in a murder hunt in the area in February, 1945. A farm labourer, Charles Walton, disappeared and his body was found apparently pinned to the ground with a hay fork and a cross carved into his chest. The famous detective, Robert Fabian of Scotland Yard, arrived to take over the investigation and, within days, had arrested an Italian prisoner of war from Long Marston. The man had been seen with blood on his hands, hiding in a ditch near the murder site. It turned out that he was just a poacher and had regularly been slipping out of the prison camp to hunt rabbits. The murder case itself is still unsolved.

### Barby Camp

Designated as Camp 1005, it was located at Willoughby, close to Rugby. Interestingly enough, there is a prison located close by, called HM Prison Onley. Whether this is the site of the original prisoner of war camp is unclear, as the prison in its current form only opened in 1968. The Barby camp was a German working camp and comparatively small.

# Wiltshire

## *Le Marchant Camp*

Camp number 23 was also designated Camp 410 and was based at Le Marchant Camp, Devizes. Camp 23 may well have been the barracks for the guards and camp 410 as the German working camp. Originally used as a transit camp, due to the enormous influxes of German prisoners of war towards the end of 1944, it became a major camp holding as many as 7,500 men. The prisoner of war camp was located about a mile from the Le Marchant barracks. In 1939, it had been used as a mustering point for British troops. The enormous numbers of Germans that were captured after the breakout in Normandy meant that trains were arriving at the site at two-hourly intervals.

There were a number of attempted escapes from this camp. One took place in December, 1944, when there was a plot by Waffen-SS officers and Fallschirmjäger apparently to seize weapons and mount an assault on London. This bizarre plot was foiled and the ringleaders were sent all the way up to Camp 21 in Scotland for the remainder of their incarceration.

## *Eastern Grey Camp*

The camp, near Malmesbury, was Camp 89. Aerial views of the site, which is now an industrial estate, clearly indicate the huts, which would have formed part of the original prisoner of war camp. It was used for German prisoners of war.

## *Eden Vale Camp*

Located in Westbury, it was known as Camp 114. There were at least three locations of prisoner of war camps in the Westbury area during the war. This particular camp, designated a German working camp, was demolished to make way for housing.

## *Military Hospital*

Lydiard Park, Purton was designated Camp 160 and also Camp 289. The park and house itself is just on the western fringes of Swindon. Much of the estate had already been broken up by the beginning of the Twentieth Century and was in a sorry state by 1939. It was requisitioned in 1941 and used initially as a US hospital. It was primarily linked to the US 101st Airborne Division. It became a prisoner of war camp shortly after the Normandy landings in 1944 and was one of the first secure accommodations for wounded enemy prisoners of war.

### Lopscombe Corner Camp
Located near Salisbury, it was designated Camp 402. This location was used as a mustering point for US troops of the 69th Infantry Division prior to the Normandy landings and subsequently used as a prisoner of war base camp.

### Ashton Gifford Camp
This was known as Camp 575 and was near Codford. Ashford Gifford House, the administrative HQ, was built from the beginning of the Nineteenth Century and was originally used as a school for pupils evacuated from Bognor Regis. In the house's history, there are no references to it being used as a prisoner of war camp, but there is an illustration drawn in 1942 by the British artist Keith Vaughan, who was a member of the Royal Pioneer Corps based at Codford, called *The Working Party*. It is reasonable to assume that some German or Italian prisoners were attached to this unit.

### Stratton Factory Camp
This was near Swindon and had been given the designations of Camp 638 and also Camp 674. This area is now effectively a part of the north east of Swindon. Stratton St Margaret also had a Vickers factory, where Spitfires were manufactured.

### Hill Camp
This was another prisoner of war camp in Westbury and designated Camp 658. There is a reference to it in *Hansard* in 1948, asking the Secretary of State for War to make the huts available at Hill Camp and Victoria Camp at Westbury available for civilian use. At that time, it was planned that there would be married

soldiers' quarters built at Victoria Camp, but Hill Camp was no longer in use. In 1942, there were Nissen huts on the Hill Camp site and, in 1943, the US Army was using it for storage purposes. They were also in the process of constructing new buildings to house around 600 servicemen. After the landings in Normandy, the camp became redundant and was used as a prisoner of war camp.

### Aliwal Barracks

Based in North Tidworth, this was designated as Camp 668. The estate here was sold to the War Department in 1897 and there was a huge amount of construction carried out so that the area could be used as barracks with attached amenities and quarters. The majority of the initial building work was carried out by 1912. During the First and Second World Wars, many Commonwealth units were stationed there. It seems likely that some of the accommodation was later used as a centre for a German working camp, although the exact location is unknown.

The Aliwal Barracks are named after the battle of Aliwal, which took place on 28th January, 1846, during the first Sikh War.

## Worcestershire

### Longbridge Camp

Longbridge Camp in Hampton Lovett, near Droitwich, was a large prisoner of war camp that was designated as Camp 54. This was a German working camp and the prisoners worked on local farms, with some being given bicycles to travel from the prison camp to the farms each day. The camp was still housing German prisoners until at least 1949. There is some evidence of the camp still in existence. It is now a residential caravan site and the hard standings for the caravans are the original footings of the prisoner of war huts.

### Recreation Ground Camp

Based at South Littleton, this was designated as Camp 277. Interestingly, this is close to HM Prison Long Lartin, which is located in South Littleton and was opened in 1971. The recreation ground had around 24 huts and was used as a German working camp.

### Fladbury Golf Course

Obviously linked to Recreation Ground Camp was Camp 277A, located on Fladbury golf course. This is actually the home of Evesham golf club, which was founded in 1894. There were Americans stationed in the area from around 1943 and the area was teeming with troops in the run up to D-Day. The golf course camp was converted into a prisoner of war camp for both Italian and German soldiers after the American servicemen left. The Germans and Italians were engaged in agricultural work, and, according to local civilians, they were identified by a large ring on the back of their uniforms. There is also another camp, listed as Camp 665 at South Littleton, listed as a German working camp.

### Perdiswell Hall

This site, near Worcester, was Camp 287. This was the former RAF Perdiswell, which had been established as an airfield in the 1930s and then requisitioned by the RAF in 1937. The hall became the HQ of No 81 Group. The prisoner of war camp was located in the area immediately around the hall in former RAF huts and operated until the end of 1947. The hall fell into disrepair and was pulled down in 1956. All that now remains are a few stone pillars, concrete bases and traces of the original landing field.

On 2nd September, 1942, an American C-47 aircraft had to force land at Perdiswell. On board was the commanding general of the USAAF, General Spaatz. Also, sitting in the co-pilot's seat, was none other than Hollywood star Clark Gable.

### Blackmore Camp

Camp 689 was in Great Malvern. Close to Lower Wyche, there is an old military road which leads to what was Blackmore prisoner of war camp. There are still water towers on the original site of this German working camp and former army camp. There are some

Blackmore Camp was a prisoner of war camp for Germans in the Second World War and a former army camp. The huge water towers, dating from the Second World War, still remain. [*Image courtesy of Trevor Rickard http://www.geograph.org.uk.*]

huts and other smaller structures remaining from the camp that was in use until 1948. Part of the camp area is now an industrial estate.

## Yorkshire

### *Gilling Camp*
Gilling Camp at Hartforth Grange was another camp designated number 4, but is also known as Camp 288. There are a number of hut platforms that still remain today. In the interwar years, Gilling Labour Camp was a camp established for the unemployed, where they worked for the Forestry Commission. From the reminiscences of prisoners of war that were held there, it was a relatively low security unit and, in fact, by Christmas 1946, those that were still there were allowed to roam within six miles of the camp.

### *Racecourse Camps*
There were several camps known as Racecourse Camp, including this one at Doncaster, designated Camp 6 and also Camp 296A, which was being used as a base camp in 1945. This may simply mean that it was essentially an administrative headquarters for prisoners that were billeted in other locations around the area.

There was another Racecourse Camp at Knavesmire near York (Camp 11). Prisoners were housed in cramped conditions in and under the grandstand and administrative centres of the racecourse which had been surrounded by barbed wire.

### *Lodge Moor Camp*
Lodge Moor Camp, Redmires Road, Sheffield was Camp 17. During the First World War it had been a major army camp. It was used during the Second World War as a prisoner of war camp for Italians, with extra tents added in order to increase capacity. There are some signs of the old camp still in existence, including part of the wall and the foundations of some of the buildings.

### *Bramham Number 1 Camp*
This was Camp 20 and situated in Boston Spa. It was a base camp and no trace of it remains today.

### Sandbeds Camp
It was situated on Gateforth New Road in Brayton. Designated as Camp 53, this standard type German working camp was thought to be unguarded, with very little barbed wire. The prisoners worked in the surrounding farms and fields. The site is now a mushroom farm.

### Overdale Camp
Located near Skipton, it had the designated number of Camp 60. The site had also been a prisoner of war camp during the First World War. During the Second World War, it initially held Italian prisoners and then became a German working camp. The camp was surrounded by barbed wire but many of the prisoners worked in the local area. The site is now a caravan park.

### Storwood Camp
Based near Cottingwith, it was designated as Camp 73. This was another German working camp that had been opened in 1940 and some isolated buildings still remain.

### Eden Camp
Situated at Old Malton, it was designated as both Camp 83 and Camp 250. This is certainly one of the few places to visit in Britain where you can see a virtually intact prisoner of war camp. There are still nearly 30 prisoner of war huts, along with mess huts and other buildings. The perimeter fence and watchtowers have been recreated and the site is now a major museum of modern history, which opened to the public in 1987. The camp was originally built in 1942 and housed Italian prisoners of war from the North African campaign. It was later extensively enlarged to hold German prisoners of war, some of whom remained there until 1948.

### Post Hill Camp
Camp 91 was in Farnley. This comprised of rooms in a former school and the Germans worked in a nearby quarry.

Eden Camp, Old Malton: this Second World War prisoner of war camp has been made into a very interesting museum. [*Image courtesy of Humphrey Bolton http://www.geograph.org.uk.*]

### Thirkleby Camp
This was designated as Camp 108 and was at Sandhill, Little Thirkleby. Thirkleby Hall and surrounding park housed a German working camp. The hall now houses a caravan site and a pig farm.

### Scriven Hall Camp
Located near Knaresborough, this was designated as both Camp 121 and 211. Scriven Hall and its parkland were used as an army camp during the war before becoming a prisoner of war camp for Germans. Local archaeologists have found a number of shell cases and mortar shell fragments. The hall itself, which had been in the Slingsby family since the Fourteenth Century, was demolished in 1952 following a fire.

### Racecourse Camp

Also designated Camp 121, there was a German working camp based on the racecourse at Ripon. It had been an important military training camp during the First World War and it took on a similar role during the Second World War. The Royal Engineers that were based there were given the freedom of the city in 1947. There were two camps based on the racecourse, designated 'North' and 'South'. The prisoner of war camp was probably closer to the old railway station. It is listed as a German working camp.

### Potter Hill Camp

Camp 127, also identified as Camp 296, was located on Potter Hill, High Green, in Sheffield. There were Italian prisoners of war in the area, but it is listed as a German working camp. It is believed that a local infant school was based around the original camp offices. By the late 1960s, all signs of the original camp had disappeared.

### High Hall Camp

Located at Bishop Burton, near Beverley, it was designated as Camp 136. This is now the site of Bishop Burton College. The estate dates back to the building of a palace for the Archbishop of York in the late-Fourteenth Century. The whole estate was requisitioned during the Second World War. The camp based here is listed as a German working camp.

### Welton House

Based in Welton Brough, this was designated as both Camp 136A and Camp 264. Allied troops stayed in Welton House and in other locations in the local area. Once these men had moved to France, it was converted into a prisoner of war camp for German prisoners. A local resident states that they had a coloured square on the back of their uniforms. The later Italian prisoners of war had a yellow diamond patch on their uniforms, and were brought to the camp after the Germans had been moved on. The camp was in the immediate vicinity of the house, in woodland.

### Butterwick Camp

This was in Boythorpe and had the designated number of Camp 159 but is also listed as Camp 163 and Camp 244. There are references to German U-boat crewmen being held here in June 1945. A German prisoner of war who was held there towards the end of the war suggests that there were around 5,000 prisoners split up into three different camps, two of which held 2,000 and one which held 1,000 men. The German prisoners were from other ranks and undertook predominantly farm work in the local area.

### Military Hospital Camp

The Military Hospital in Naburn, York was given the designation of Camp 162. Naburn Hospital was opened as York's asylum in 1906. During the Second World War, the army requisitioned the hospital and a larger military hospital was constructed in the grounds, with numerous huts. The main hospital was returned to normal use in 1942 but the hutted hospital continued to be used and, in 1947, became a prisoner of war camp. It was not until the early 1950s that the buildings were emptied and taken over again by the NHS. The hospital closed in 1988 whereupon all of the buildings were demolished and a shopping outlet was opened in 1998.

### Weston Lane Camp

Based in Otley, this was designated as Camp 164. This was also designated Camp 245. A watercolour, which was painted by a German prisoner of war in 1945, shows a tented camp. The German prisoners of war seem to have begun arriving in 1944 and it closed in late 1948. Two German prisoners of war tried to escape and were shot as they crossed the perimeter wires. The men were buried in Otley cemetery, along with five others who died of other causes during their imprisonment, but subsequently moved to the German military cemetery in Cannock Chase which opened in 1964. All that remains of the camp is a gateway.

## Dog and Duck Cottage
Located at Norton-in-Malton, near the bigger Eden Camp, it was known as Camp 172.

## Urebank Camp
Situated in Ripon, it was designated Camp 178 and is also listed as Camp 247. There is now a caravan park on this site, although there are several concrete pads of the large number of huts were once on the original site of what is listed as both a base camp and a working camp for German prisoners of war. Prior to its use as a prisoner of war camp, it was used as a transit camp for Allied units waiting postings overseas or to alternative camps in Britain.

## Butcher Hill
This camp at Horsforth was Camp 244 and Camp 245. This camp was a large, purpose-built one with around 500 prisoners, and was also responsible for the administration of other smaller camps in the area, housing between 100 and 200 prisoners at each.

## Norton Camp
This site on Cinder Hill Lane in Norton was designated as Camp 248 and was a German working camp. It is of interest that there was an aerodrome called RAF Norton, which was used as a detention centre for bomber crews who had shown what was coined as 'lack of courage or moral fibre'. The prisoner of war camp was not actually based on the RAF airfield but was situated close by.

## Thorpe Hall
Camp 250 was in Rudston. The hall is believed to date back to the middle of the Seventeenth Century. Although the main camp was in the woods opposite the main entrance to Thorpe Hall, there were other parts of the camp outside the village of Rudston. The camp bakery was on Eastgate.

## Ravensfield Park Camp
This was designated as Camp 296 and was near Rotherham. This was a German working camp and the men worked at a colliery in

Rotherham. The camp was centred round Ravensfield Hall and, initially, there were Italian prisoners of war in brown uniforms with yellow circles on their backs. It was open between 1945 and 1947.

### Stable Road Camp
This camp in Barlow was given the number 564. There was an ordnance depot here that was used to store bombs prior to being delivered to the airfields in the area. The site also has associations with the First World War when there was an airship construction yard based there. In other sources, this is listed as a Royal Navy ordnance depot.

### Searchlight Site Camp
Camp 585 was Searchlight Site Camp at Husthwaite. Originally, this was the site of a Home Guard, Searchlight and Lewis gun team. Nothing now remains of the camp.

### Stadium Camp
Located in Catterick, it was designated Camp 631, but is also listed as Camp 662 and Camp 664. Catterick has a long association with the military and it had been used as a prisoner of war camp during the First World War, holding some 5,000 prisoners. A German working camp was established there in the Second World War.

### Cowick Hall
This site in West Cowick, Snaith was designated Camp 636 and Camp 691. The hall was built in the late Seventeenth Century. The hall was empty at the beginning of the Second World War and, towards the end of the war, it became a German working camp. The hall is still in existence but there are no remains of the camp as the parkland was restored.

### Centenary Road
Based in Goole, this had the number Camp 637. There were quite a few huts at this camp but very little in the way of security. The German prisoners of war worked on the land and, in particular, were involved in land drainage.

**Thomas Street**

This site in Selby was Camp 690 and had links with the Sandbeds Camp (53), Brayton in Selby. It is listed as a small German working camp.

**RAF Burn Airfield**

There was another camp in the Selby area, based on the former RAF Burn airfield. This was designated Camp 1007 and was a vehicle depot. RAF Burn had been opened in 1942 but, by July 1945, it had effectively been closed. Some of the airfield buildings were later used to house a German working camp.

**Station Road**

Another camp in the Selby area, it was based in Tadcaster. The German working camp was designated Camp 1015.

# Chapter Three

# Locations in the Rest of the British Isles

## NORTHERN IRELAND

THERE were several prisoner of war camps established in Northern Ireland that operated between 1944 and around 1948. It has been estimated that around two per cent of all German prisoners of war held in Britain were actually in camps in Northern Ireland, roughly 13,000 men.

### County Antrim

#### *Lissanoure Camp*

The Lissanoure Camp at Loughgiel was designated Camp 190. This was based around Lissanoure Castle, which was built towards the end of the Twelfth Century. The estate was used to billet US troops during the Second World War and, after the surrender of Germany in May 1945, a prisoner of war camp was established here to hold German U-boat crews.

### County Armagh

#### *Gosford Camp*

This was given the designated number of Camp 10 and was at Gosford Castle. The castle's construction began in 1819 but it was not completed until the 1850s. During the Second World War, it was used as a prisoner of war base camp. During the war, the castle was also used by US Army artillery, the Royal Artillery and the

Pioneer Corps. Later, it was acquired by the Forestry Commission. There are the remains of a windmill on the site, which was built by German prisoners of war, as well as some concrete bases of Nissen huts still visible and short sections of concrete paths that used to belong to the camp.

### Elmfield Camp

Camp 11 was the Elmfield Camp at Gilford, near Portadown and was also designated Camp 12. Field Marshal Montgomery's mother was a regular visitor to the camp as she worked for the Red Cross and also attended the local church. There are traces that there was a prisoner of war camp located in the Brownstown area of Portadown, although the main prisoner of war camp was located at the top of Dixon's Hill, primarily on what was called the Polo Field. The camp held around 1,800 prisoners of war and extended as far as the road to Lurgan. There were not only German prisoners of war but also Italians housed there. The men are described as wearing khaki uniforms with a yellow diamond patch on their backs. The majority of the men were either from the army or the air force. Four prisoners escaped in the early months of 1945. Two of them were captured fairly quickly, and had been planning to get to Southern Ireland. The other two men were picked up on the border with Southern Ireland, which was neutral during the Second World War. The prisoner of war camp closed during 1948 and the camp huts were auctioned off, including one which contained a hidden escape map. There is very little left of the camp, apart from some old septic tanks.

## County Down

### Holywood Camp

This camp in Belfast was designated variously as Camp 14, Camp 172 and Camp 682. There are a number of potential sites around the Belfast area for this camp. Holywood Camp had an annexe at Orangefield and there was also a subsidiary camp on what was the Balmoral Golf Club. This camp is now a housing estate. The Orangefield camp was, in fact, a military hospital and was located in Orangefield Primary School. Some of the German prisoners of war, amongst whom were naval and army personnel, who died there are buried in Belfast City Cemetery.

### Rockport Camp
This was Camp 173. Crumlin Road Gaol, which was built in 1845, was also used to house prisoners of war. In 1940 the prison ship, *Al Rawdah*, was moored near Killyleagh, before the prisoners were transferred to the gaol in 1941. There was also an escape by five prisoners in 1941 when part of the prison wall was demolished during an air raid. Rockport was a former RAF camp, but it also served as a prisoner of war base camp and had two further designations, Camp 681 and, like Holywood Camp, was also designated Camp 682.

### County Tyrone

### Monrush Camp
This was designated as Camp 5 and was situated at Cookstown. Cookstown was a major army base and was later used by the US Army. There was a large internment camp established here, which later became a base camp for German prisoners of war. Amongst the US troops stationed in the Cookstown area were elements of the 505th Parachute Infantry Regiment of the 82nd Airborne Division. After they departed for Normandy, the camp was converted into a prisoner of war camp.

### Dungannon Camp
Camp 187 was at Dungannon. The US 8th Infantry Division were based in Dungannon Park and other locations in the area. The British 59th Division were also stationed there. Later, elements of the US 34th Infantry Division were located in Dungannon. There was a prisoner of war camp in Dungannon Park. There are a number of huts still remaining of a prisoner of war camp at Ballynorthland. Prior to it being used as a prisoner of war camp, it was used by a US field artillery observation unit for a short while.

### Lisnelly Camp

The military barracks at Lisnelly, Omagh was also used as a prisoner of war camp. Camp 190 was based at Cloughmills. There is another camp also given the designation 190 which is identified as being at Cloughmills in County Antrim.

## SCOTLAND

During the First World War, there were around 25 prisoner of war camps or internment camps in Scotland. There were at least 20 during the Second World War.

## Aberdeenshire

### Stuartfield Camp

Camp 110 was at Stuartfield Camp, Mintlaw Station. The earliest prisoners of war at this camp were Italians, however, later, most of the 500 prisoners held there were Germans captured during the

The old gateposts at the old prisoner of war camp at Stuartfield in Aberdeenshire remain, as do some of the now derelict huts. [*Image courtesy of Iain Smith http://www.geograph.org.uk.*]

Normandy campaign. The bulk of the prisoners of war taken in Normandy belonged to the 12th Panzer Division, who were captured after the battles around Caen. The site is listed as a German working camp. Shortly after the war, the camp was used to house displaced Eastern Europeans. The camp was used until the early 1950s. Although several of the original buildings were demolished, a good number still remain, including remnants of a stone gateway. There is also a water tower on the site.

### Deer Park Camp

This was designated as Camp 111 and was at Monymusk. This 25-acre site could hold 1,300 prisoners of war in a mix of 20 or so huts and nearly 70 tents. Italian prisoners of war were first held at the site, they worked on local farms and were carried about in the local area by trucks. The Italians or possibly the Ukrainians held there made a chapel with an elaborate altar out of one of the huts. The camp became a German working camp in around 1945, when German prisoners of war were being brought back from North America. The camp became a centre for Polish and other Eastern European refugees after the war and it is believed that the camp was finally levelled in the 1980s and is now beneath St Ninian's housing estate.

In 2003, when plans began to build on a site to the east of Brucklay Castle, the remains of a prisoner of war camp was discovered. Up to 35 concrete bases were still there. It would appear that the huts were separated into three groups with pathways between them. Further investigation suggested that the camp actually spread further into newly-planted woodland to the south and the west of the site. Brucklay Castle itself was sold off in 1952 and many of the original features were sold for reclamation.

### Tullos Hill

Located in Aberdeen, this is listed as a camp for German prisoners of war in the post-war period. The site was also used by an anti-aircraft battery. Until recently, the area was used as a landfill site, but in 2009, the remains of the camp were discovered. There were at least two other camps in Aberdeen, one in Hayton and the other in Peterculter. Both sites are now lost under later buildings. The Hayton Road site consisted of a number of Nissen huts and was quite large. The Peterculter site housed Italian prisoners of war. It was located opposite the Aberdeen waterworks tower and was a barbed wire enclosure with huts and an attached football field.

## Angus

### *Kinnell Camp*
Kinnell Camp, Friockheim, near Arbroath, was designated Camp 275 and Camp 275A. Aerial photographs that were taken in April 1946 show six huts and a rectangular area with paths. The actual site of the camp is to the east of the Friockheim cemetery. The camp housed Italians to begin with and there is local talk that there was a marble altar made and used by them.

### *Tealing Airfield*
This was used as a prisoner of war camp. The RAF mothballed the airfield in 1945. The airfield's most famous visitor was the Russian Foreign Minister Molotov who landed at the airfield en route to Chequers to meet Winston Churchill on 20th May, 1942. He had the choice of two aircraft for the onward flight south. The one that he did not choose crashed in the Vale of York, killing some of his entourage and the RAF crew.

## Argyll

### *Glenbranter Camp*
This was designated as Camp 6 and was in the grounds of Glenbranter House. In the 1930s, a work camp for the young unemployed was set up in the grounds. The prisoner of war camp was originally used to hold Italian prisoners, and was located on either side of the drive leading to the house. There were some 17 huts to the north and 14 to the south. Prior to it becoming a prisoner of war camp, it had also been used as a training base for landing craft signalmen.

It is worth noting that Glenbranter House was the home of the music hall star, Harry Lauder (1870–1950).

### Knapdale Camp
It had the designation of Camp 24 and was situated in a rural part of Argyll and Bute. In the 1930s, an instructional centre was set up for the unemployed, one of some 38 such centres across Britain. During the Second World War, it was converted into a prisoner of war camp. In fact, one inmate was a Japanese prisoner of war. His background was confusing and it seems possible that he may have been a merchant seaman on a British ship that was subsequently interned when Japan entered the war. He died at Knapdale camp and is buried at Achnabreac in Argyll.

## Ayrshire

### Doonfoot Camp
Situated in Ayr, it was designated as Camp 14. In the 20th December, 1944 edition of the *Glasgow Herald* there was a short piece regarding the capture of 11 Italian prisoners of war. The Dunure village policeman heard about some strangers near a railway line close by and found six escaped Italian prisoners of war in a hut. Meanwhile, the Maybole police had picked up four more and another had been captured elsewhere. In all, 97 Italian prisoners of war had tunnelled out of the camp, but it is believed that all of them were recaptured. Later, in May of 1945, the Gordon Highlanders were involved with the Doonfoot Camp. They were responsible for escorting around 500 German prisoners of war who were employed to carry out menial duties in the local area, including putting up marquees for garden fêtes and working in the Gordon Highlander's dining room as orderlies.

### Pennylands Camp
This was designated as Camp 22 and was near Cumnock. Pennylands Barracks was built on the estate of Dumfries House and, in 1942, was requisitioned. It became a prisoner of war camp

as early as 1943. By 1944, it had become a repatriation centre for displaced Polish refugees and remained in this role until 1947.

## Kingencleugh Camp

Camp 112 was Kingencleugh Camp near Mauchline. This is listed as a German working camp, although we know that Polish civilians and soldiers were situated here after the war. The story of this camp is fairly familiar: first housing Italians and later Germans who worked on local farms. There were around 500 prisoners of war here.

## Maidens/Kirkoswald Camp

Maidens or Kirkoswald Camp is unlisted and does not have a camp number. It lies to the north of Girvan on the coast road. Aerial photographs show the camp, which was associated with RAF Turnberry, another site which housed Italian prisoners of war and also Lithuanian prisoners who had fought on the side of the Germans.

## Banffshire

## Sandyhillock Camp

Based at Craigellachie, it was designated as Camp 67. Some 39 Nissen huts were located in a rectangular perimeter area, according to an aerial photograph dated August 1946. Across the road were another 27 huts for guards and administrative personnel. The site is now a poultry farm and some of the huts are used for chickens.

## Duff House

This is another Scottish prisoner of war camp that is not listed with a camp number. It was located in Banff on the site of what is now the Duff House Royal Golf Course. The original house was designed by William Adam and was built in the 1730s. The house was used as a hotel, army billet, sanatorium and, later, as a prisoner of war camp.

Duff himself is said to have actually hated the place after arguments during its construction. The situation had got so bad that he could not bear even to look at the place and never lived there. It is said that, whenever he passed within sight of the house, he pulled down the blinds of his carriage.

## Berwickshire

### Ninewells Camp

This German working camp was designated as Camp 236 and was near Chirnside, within the grounds of Ninewells House. The original building was constructed in the Eighteenth Century, but was rebuilt in the middle of the Nineteenth Century. It operated as a prisoner of war camp from 1942 but was later used as a hostel for Eastern European displaced persons, including Polish soldiers.

## Borders

### Stobs Camp

This site near Hawick is not listed with a camp number. However, it has a long association with holding prisoners of war. In October 1914, it was decided that some 200 huts would be constructed on the site in order to hold around 6,000 enemy prisoners of war. During the Second World War, only a few German prisoners were actually held there. They arrived towards the end of the war and were held in a stockade at Howdenbank called Wilton Camp.

### Leet Water

The other unnumbered camp in the area was Leet Water, near Coldstream. Aerial photographs taken in 1946 reveal the location of the camp, which was on the west bank of Leet Water, to the northwest of Lees Farm and the site is now a golf course. In the corner of a field, there were nine huts. The hut location is roughly where the golf club house is now situated. Italians were held here under fairly lax security and were allowed to work on local farms. Locals call the site Tally Hill.

## Caithness

### Watten Camp

Located at Watten, near Wick, it was designated Camp 165. Although this is listed as a base camp, it would appear that this was used as a denazification site. It had a high level of security and only the most dangerous of the German prisoners of war were interned there. The site remained open until at least 1948, having opened in 1943. The camp was split into two distinct areas. The first area was a regular German prisoner of war base camp but the second area was used to house the more dangerous, so-called black German prisoners of war. This part of the camp had watchtowers and a double wire enclosure. Several prominent Nazis were held here, including former concentration camp guards, fanatical Waffen-SS and U-boat captains.

## Dumfriesshire

### Barony Camp

Situated in Dumfries on the estate of Kirkmichael House, this was designated as Camp 182 and also as Camp 298. The guards and administrative area was to the northeast of the house, with the prisoner of war camp located to the northwest. This comprised 90 or so Nissen huts. Many of the buildings were demolished when the camp was closed.

### Halmuir Farm Camp

This had the designation of Camp 68 and was situated near Halmuir, Lockerbie. There is a Ukrainian-built camp chapel still in existence at this site and some of the other huts are still visible.

### Carronbridge Camp

The German working camp at Carronbridge, to the northeast of Drumlanrig Castle, was Camp 293. There were a considerable number of huts here, with nearly 60 of them as part of the prisoner of war camp and a further 26 for guards and other personnel. There was also a perimeter fence around the site. There is a copy of a sports day programme dated June 1947, which includes a brief history of the camp. At its peak, the camp held 1,000 men, had a theatre, a hospital, a church and a library and there was a regular camp newspaper. The men wore brown work clothes and worked largely in farm labouring jobs. A number of the men did not return home to Germany and married locally. Others had their wives and families brought to Scotland. There is an interesting story that one of the more elderly former prisoners was still living in his hut on the camp until the late 1960s. A sewage works is now located on part of the site.

### Honduras Camp
This German working camp was designated as Camp 612 and was near Kirkpatrick Fleming. What is interesting about this is that there is a cemetery at Kirkpatrick Fleming that has seven war graves, including four members of the British Honduras Forestry Unit who had been recruited from the Caribbean colony to help the British war effort. The prisoner of war camp was located next to the camp of the Honduran foresters who were repatriated early because of poor living conditions and their difficulty in adjusting to the harsh climate.

### Dryffeholme Camp
Camp 617 was near Lockerbie. There were a number of huts visible from aerial photographs taken in 1948. The camp, consisting of at least 150 predominantly Nissen huts, was spread from Halleaths House to an abandoned railway and was established around June 1941.

### Isles House Stables
An unnumbered camp was located at the Isles House Stables in Kirkcudbright and was used for a limited period of time to house Italian prisoners of war.

## Dunbartonshire

### Blairvadach Camp

Camp 582 was Blairvadach Camp, near Helensburgh. This was a German working camp comprising of around 40 huts. The camp was sited to the southwest of the estate that used to belong to Blairvadach House.

### Stukenduff Camp

Closely associated, at least geographically, to this Blairvadach Camp was the Stukenduff base camp, designated as Camp 230. Although nothing remains of the camp which has since had a road and housing built on it, it originally held 60 Nissen huts.

## East Lothian

### Gosford Camp

Camp 16 was Gosford Camp, Aberlady. Gosford House was taken over as accommodation for troops in 1940. By 1944, it had become a prisoner of war camp and could accommodate 3,000 prisoners. It soon became overcrowded and a second camp at Amisfield, close to Haddington, was set up and designated Camp 16A.

### Amisfield Camp

This sub-camp, also designated as Camp 243, was predominantly non-German, with a considerable number of Austrian prisoners of war. The camp stayed open for around two years, after which the men were sent back to Gosford Camp. The Amisfield camp was then used to house Ukrainian prisoners of war who had been captured in German uniform.

Amisfield Park had a Palladian mansion dating from the 1750s, which was demolished in 1928. In the First World War, the site was requisitioned by the army and used as a headquarters for the Lothian and Border Horse Regiment. When a local builder bought it in 1923, the stone and bricks were used to build a school, a hospital and other buildings. In the Second World War, the park area was used by the Sherwood Foresters and then by Polish troops before it became a prisoner of war camp.

## Fife

### *Annsmuir Camp*
Annsmuir Camp at Ladybank was Camp 77. Construction for this camp started in 1942. Originally, it was intended that part of the camp should be tented and the rest covered with huts. There would also be a detention block, cookhouse and reception station. The site now contains the Ladybank Golf Course and a caravan park.

### *Bonnytown Camp*
This was a small prisoner of war camp. The camp itself was located to the southwest of the Bonnytown farmhouse and was used to house Italian prisoners of war. A few of the huts, made of pre-cast concrete, remained on the site until they were demolished in 2004 as they were in a poor state of repair. There were also other small buildings.

### *Capeldrae, Westfield*
Capeldrae, Westfield near Ballingry is an area closely associated with coal mines. There may have been a Bevin Boy camp in the area that is rumoured to have been used as a prisoner of war camp. There was certainly one of these Bevin Boy camps in Comrie, Fife and many of the buildings exist to this day.

---

**Bevin Boys**
Bevin Boy Camps are named after the Minister of Labour, Ernest Bevin. He masterminded the scheme, which ran between 1943–48, to conscript young men to work for the war effort by sending them down the pits instead of into the armed forces. Around 48,000 men were recruited.

---

## Kincardineshire

### North Hill Camp
This was designated both as Camp 75 and Camp 76. It was near Laurencekirk. In 1946 Canadian soldiers, belonging to the Veteran's Guard of Canada, were guarding the camp. These men had already fought in the First World War and were used like a Home Guard, guarding power plants and prisoner of war camps or other places/businesses vital to the war effort. The site is now a housing estate.

## Kirkcudbrightshire

### St Andrew's Hall
St Andrew's Hall, St Mary's Isle, was designated as Camp 640. This is a narrow peninsular near the River Dee. The general area of Kirkcudbright was used by the British Army from 1942 and through the D-Day landings in 1944. St Andrew's Hall was a Roman Catholic building and did not house a large number of prisoners of war.

## Midlothian

### Woodhouselee Camp
This prisoner of war camp was at Milton Bridge and was Camp 2. It was used as a working camp and was clearly visible from aerial photographs taken in 1946. The camp has been returned to farmland.

### Donaldson School
Based in West Coates, Edinburgh, it was given the designation of Camp 12. This was built as a hospital in the 1850s and was used as a military hospital during the First World War. In 1938, it became a school for deaf children. As a prisoner of war camp during the Second World War, it housed both Italian and German prisoners. The school moved out of its original building in 2008 to a new campus in Linlithgow.

William Henry Playfair (1790–1857) designed Donaldson School which was used as a prisoner of war camp in the Second World War. Queen Victoria was, apparently, so jealous, saying that it outclassed some of her own palaces. [*Image courtesy of Sandy Gemmill www.geograph.org.uk.*]

### Inchdrewer House
The house on Colinton Road, Edinburgh was the location of Camp 105 and housed a German working party. Interestingly, Inchdrewer House is now the Army School of Bagpipe Music and Highland Drumming. The house itself was built in the Sixteenth Century.

### Dalmahoy Camp
Camp 123 was Dalmahoy Camp. This is believed to have been situated on the former airfield, RAF Kirknewton. It was originally established as an airfield in 1940 but it was switched over to use as a prisoner of war camp, as a transit camp for German officers en route to North American prisoner of war camps. The military camp where the prisoner of war camp was sited, was to the southwest of the airfield. There were almost 40 huts there. RAF Kirknewton was listed as a contingency hospital in 1991 and was still in use in the recent past. It is believed that the CIA and the US Air Force used the site to intercept Russian signals.

## Duddingston Camp

An aerial photograph taken by the RAF in April 1946 shows the site, which is close to the Dalmahoy Camp, marked as being between the Duddingston golf course and the Duddingston Road West. The centre of the camp was around a drill ground, which is now part of the grounds of a school. The camp also extended into the grounds of Duddingston House, which is now a hotel. There were a number of Nissen huts, plus some larger wooden buildings. The camp spread out across either side of the railway tracks at Duddingston Junction. It was also used after the war as a camp for displaced persons.

## Deer Park Camp

Camp 1013 or 1024 was called Deer Park Camp, near Dalkeith. Lying just five miles from Edinburgh, this is now a country park. This is listed as two German working camps but there were, in fact, three distinct areas of huts. The main areas of huts were located to the east and the southeast of Cat Hough where there were around 40 huts.

The Eskmill, built in Dalkeith in 1775, was the first cotton mill in Scotland. During the Napoleonic Wars, it was used as the barracks for British troops guarding the 6,000 French prisoners of war held at Valleyfield.

## Mortonhall

Photographs from the air show signs that this Edinburgh site was once a prisoner of war camp, then used for displaced or interned people. The area, which is now a holiday camp, still has the concrete bases which were laid for the old, wartime huts.

## The Orkney Islands

## Warebanks Camp

Camp 34 was at Kirkwall, on Burray and was used to house Italian prisoners of war who were captured in North Africa.

The Italian prisoners of war built chapels at both Warebanks Camp and Lamb Holm on the Orkney Islands. The one at Lamb Holm still remains and was created from two Nissen huts. [*Image courtesy of Gregory J. Kingsley.*]

### Lamb Holm

It was originally intended that all of the prisoners shipped to the Orkney Islands would stay at Camp 34 but, in fact, 500 of them were shifted to Camp 60 at Lamb Holm. The Italian prisoners built chapels at both sites but the one at Camp 34 no longer exists as it was demolished in 1945. The prisoners at Lamb Holm constructed the Italian chapel from two Nissen huts. At Lamb Holm, it is also possible to see hut bases, air raid shelters and a tramway that was used to move stone to construct a pier.

The remains of Prisoner of War Camp 60, Lamb Holm on Orkney. [*Image courtesy of Nicholas Mutton http://www.geograph.org.uk.*]

### The Rockworks Camp

This camp on Rerwick Head on Orkney consisted of a number of huts and roadways. The site was near the Commodore Hotel and the nearby bungalows. From an aerial photograph taken in 1942, there were several large shed-like buildings that were used for quarrying operations. The accommodation consisted of around 18 huts. Italian prisoners were held here from around 1942.

## Perthshire

### Balhary Camp

Camp 3 was Balhary Camp and it was also listed as Camp 63. The camp near Balhary still existed in the late-1990s. It was also used to house displaced persons and was a large camp with some 35 huts inside a fenced compound and a further 20 or more huts that were used as offices and accommodation for the guards.

A wall painting inside one of the prisoner of war huts at Balhary Camp. [*Image courtesy of Elliot Simpson http://www.geograph.org.uk.*]

One of two wall paintings inside one of the prisoner of war huts which was painted by one of the prisoners. [*Image courtesy of Elliot Simpson http://www. geograph.org.uk.*]

Some of the huts featured here at Balhary Camp have since been destroyed. [*Image courtesy of Elliot Simpson http://www.geograph.org.uk.*]

### *Comrie Camp*

Based in Comrie, it was designated as Camp 21. This had originally been set up as Cultybraggan Camp in 1941. The camp was split into five compounds and was used as a maximum security camp for unrepentant Nazi prisoners of war. In December 1944, the inmates murdered a prisoner because they believed him to be a British spy. Five of the German prisoners were subsequently tried and executed for the murder. All of the 2,000 officers at the camp were split up and distributed to other camps and Comrie was closed down.

It remained under the ownership of the Ministry of Defence until 2004. Fearing that it would be used for redevelopment, local residents bought the site. In the post-war period, it was used as a training camp and, in recent years, some of the Nissen huts have been refurbished for local businesses. This camp is one of the best examples of an intact prisoner of war camp. There are a number of the original huts still in existence and the buildings are now listed properties.

Cultybraggan Camp was constructed in 1941 as a Prisoner of War camp. Thirty-one of the buildings, the majority of them being Nissen huts, are Category A listed by Historic Scotland. [*Image courtesy of Mick Garratt http://www.geograph.org.uk.*]

### Calvine Camp

Camp 66 was Calvine Camp, at Blair Atholl. The prisoners here were held in a square perimeter with around 38 huts. To the northwest of the prison compound was a similar number of huts. There was an interesting answer to a question posed in the House of Commons on 30th July, 1946 regarding Calvine Camp. It stated that the men had a bread and flour ration of 74oz a week if they were not working, and 135 if they were working. Polish refugees were still residing in the camp in the 1950s.

### Cowden Camp

Camp 242 was in Comrie. Some 33 Nissen huts were set inside a rectangular barbed wire perimeter here, with 14 or so other buildings used by guards and administrative personnel. It was designated a German working camp.

## Errol Airfield

This was designated as Camp 274. RAF Errol was opened in January 1943 with three runways and six hangars. It closed as an airfield in 1948. The control tower still survives, as do a number of the huts closest to the road. Part of the airfield was used a prisoner of war camp, listed as a working camp.

## Methven Airfield

The Methven Airfield (also known as Loanleven) was used as a maintenance airfield until 1944. The whole site was spread out over three fields, with the headquarters building to the west of the grass runway. The site itself is close to Methven Castle and Loch. The RAF accommodation huts were a mix of Nissen huts and wooden structures, which were positioned in woodland. The site itself opened in 1940 and was used initially for the repair of aircraft. In 1944, the accommodation buildings became a prisoner of war camp. Italians were the first to be housed there and, later, German prisoners. It was not surrounded by barbed wire and the majority of the prisoners had already left the site by the end of 1945.

# Renfrewshire

## Patterton Camp

Based near Thornliebank, it was designated Camp 660. This camp is near Glasgow and was used initially to house Italian prisoners of war and later Germans. Once these had been repatriated, the camp became a centre for the Polish Resettlement Corp until around 1949. The majority of the 70 or so huts were demolished in 1960. The camp was used during the First World War by troops from Australia and New Zealand. Vintage aerial photographs show that there was a parade square, a football pitch and vegetable allotments. Italian prisoners of war were held there from around May 1944 until the last left the camp a year later. It became a German working camp and the prisoners not only worked on local farms but were also deployed in a local printworks. The site is now covered with housing and a country park.

**Ross**

*Brahan Castle*
Situated in Dingwall, to the north of Inverness, this was Camp 109.
A handful of Nissen huts and evidence of concrete pads and paths
are still visible here. The castle was built in 1611 and was briefly
requisitioned during the Second World War. The castle was
demolished in the early 1950s but it was from Brahan Castle that
the Seaforth Highlanders were raised. All that survives of the castle
today at Brahan is an ornamental wall. The prisoner of war camp
is listed as a German working camp.

**Roxburghshire**

*Sunlaws Camp*
Based in Kelso, it was designated as Camp 120 and was listed as a
German working camp.

**South Lanarkshire**

*Happendon Camp*
This was designated Camp 19. In fact two camps were given this
number, the second being Douglas Castle. There were three
prisoner of war camps in this immediate area, which were open
from around 1944 to 1946. Part of the Happendon Camp was
transformed into what is believed to be the first family-owned
motorway service station.

*The Moor Camp*
Based at Thankerton, it was designated as Camp 62. This is listed
as a German working camp and the only remnant of this camp that
still remains is a property known as the Thankerton Camp Farm.

**Stirlingshire**

*Castle Rankine Camp*
Camp 64 was at Castle Rankine, Denny, near Falkirk. The castle,
also known as Gertranky, dated from the Thirteenth Century but

has long since been destroyed. The main prison camp that was here consisted of around 39 huts for the prisoners and an additional 24 for the guards and administrative personnel. It is understood that most of the area is now a pig farm. Some of the German prisoners of war who had been captured on D-Day, then sent to America, were later shipped back to Britain and held at Camp 64 until around December 1948. The camp also held Italian prisoners of war.

### Abbey Craig Park

This site at Causeway Head in Stirling was designated as Camp 559.

Abbey Craig Park prisoner of war camp was close to the imposing Wallace Monument, which was built between 1861 and 1869 in honour of Sir William Wallace who was executed after attempting to re-establish Scotland's independence during the reign of King Edward I (1272–1307). [*Image courtesy of Finlay McWalter.*]

## Sutherland

### *Earl's Cross House*

This was designated Camp 641 and was at Dornoch. According to an aerial photograph taken in May 1946, the small prisoner of war camp was located to the east of Earl's Cross House. Only around seven or eight huts are visible in the photograph. The house is an early-Twentieth Century Arts and Crafts building. Associated with this camp was a second site on the Golf Road at Dornoch. This site was photographed from the air in 1946 and seems to be centred on Church Street. It consisted of around 20 huts. The German working camp is now beneath post-war homes.

## Wigtownshire

### *Holm Park Camp*

This was designated as Camp 113 and was at Newton Stewart. The camp was used to house Italian prisoners of war initially but, when they were repatriated, the camp predominantly housed German army and air force personnel as a German working camp. It then became a camp for Czech and Polish refugees. The site became a campsite in 1964, but there are still some traces of the original camp, including the roads that were built by the Italians, a storage room, a tower and a reception building. There was also reported to be a telephone box that had been converted from a sentry box.

### *ST2*

Camp 571 was in Stranraer.

### *Leffnoll*

Another Stranraer-based camp was 661, near Cairnryan. This was originally a military camp and the men were engaged in work on the military railway. Aerial photographs reveal the outlines of the camp. It would appear that there were around 27 huts for guards and administration staff and then another 73 inside a perimeter area. The original camp was made considerably larger before it became a prisoner of war camp.

At the end of the Second World War, the port of Cairnryan was used to deal with nearly 90 German U-boats that had been surrendered, and the port also handled the breaking up of Royal Navy vessels such as *HMS Ark Royal*. The port was closed in 1959 and the railway was pulled up in 1967.

## Culreoch Camp
Another Stranraer camp was on the site of the former anti-aircraft battery situated to protect Loch Ryan. The actual site is to the northeast of Whiteleys Farm where there were four gun emplacements. In an aerial photograph taken in 1946, there is an accommodation camp, command post and tracks. At the time, there were still 10 Nissen huts on the site and the concrete foundations for another 16. The site was used to house Italians.

## Sheuchan School
The school in Stranraer was also used as a transit camp for prisoners. During the war, the school, which had closed in 1938, was used by the ARP.

## WALES

## Anglesey

## Camp 32
Camp 32 was on Anglesey.

## Breconshire

## Talgarth Hospital
This was designated as Camp 234. This former asylum was requisitioned as a military mental hospital in 1940. At this stage of the war, the hospital had a capacity of just over 300 beds. Towards the end of the war, the military section of the Talgarth became a prisoner of war hospital for Italian and German prisoners. The hospital was closed in 2000 and the building is now semi-derelict.

## Caernarvonshire

### Pablo Hall Camp
This was at Llandudno Junction and was designated as Camp 119. Although listed as being a German working camp, the site also housed Italian prisoners up until 1944.

## Carmarthenshire

### Henllan Bridge Farm Camp
Based near Llandyssul, this was designated as Camp 70. The camp was built between 1941 and 1942 and housed primarily Italian prisoners. It is thought that the camp had a capacity of between 1,000 and 1,500 prisoners. This was an extensive camp and included 35 huts, a hospital, kitchens, offices, a theatre and sports facilities.

Built to house Italian prisoners in the Second World War, the former Henllan Bridge Farm prisoner of war camp is now used for industrial units. [*Image courtesy of Marion Phillips http://www.geograph.org.uk.*]

The prisoner quarters were encircled by administrative offices and billets for the guards. During their time at this camp, some of the Italian prisoners requested permission to build their own Catholic church. During 1944, they turned one of the huts into an ornate place of worship using corned beef tins, old Red Cross boxes, fruit, vegetables, tea leaves, fish bones and cocoa tins to create the altar, pillars and candlesticks. The chapel was named The Church of the Sacred Heart and can still be viewed, although the former camp is now the site of industrial storage facilities.

### Llanddarog Camp
Camp 102 is listed as a German working camp and the prisoners would work on local farms. The camp had a perimeter fence, sentry boxes and single-storey buildings.

### Ystrad Camp
Camp 199 was Ystrad Camp in Carmarthen. The prisoner of war camp was housed on the former base occupied by British and American forces. The site is now the home of a large housing and industrial estate.

### Abergwili (Glangwili) Hospital
This was designated as Camp 252. The site had originally been built to deal with American casualties but it was transformed into a prisoner of war camp towards the end of the Second World War. This is now the location of the West Wales General Hospital.

## Denbighshire

### Pool Park Camp
Located near Ruthin, it had the designated number of Camp 38. Initially, it was a camp for Italian prisoners of war and there is still a small amount of physical evidence in existence. The prisoners worked on local farms, nurseries and craft works. By 1946, the camp housed German prisoners until their repatriation in 1948.

## Flintshire

### The Ordnance Storage Depot

The Ordnance Storage Depot at Queensferry in the Alyn Valley was designated as Camp 1014. This former lead mining area was requisitioned in 1939 and developed as a chemical weapons factory and storage area, producing predominantly mustard gas weapons. There were in excess of 100 buildings constructed on the site during the Second World War, in addition to an extensive rail infrastructure.

## Glamorganshire

### Island Farm Camp

This site in Bridgend was known as Camp 198. It is probably best known for the escape attempt that took place on the night of 10th–11th March, 1945, when 70 German prisoners of war tunnelled out of the camp and scattered across Britain. Camp 198 was originally opened in order to house people working in the Royal Ordnance Factory. As it transpired, the majority of the workers did not want to remain housed in the camp and, for the most part, it was empty until US troops began arriving in the area in October 1943. Numerous units preparing for the Normandy landings were housed here, notably the 28th US Infantry Division, which comprised three infantry regiments, along with supporting formations. Island Farm took possession of its first German officers in November 1944. From the outset, they were uncooperative, particularly given the fact that they had to march the last two miles from the nearest railway station. A lot of these men were considered to be high risk and, as such, security was supposed to be tight. But a tunnel was discovered in January 1945, extending out of Hut 16.

The camp itself was an extensive affair and the site can be found alongside the A48 on the road from Cardiff to Port Talbot. As was normally the case, part of the camp was given over to the camp's guards but, in addition to this, there were other distinct areas with specific purposes. The main area, which consisted of huts used for sleeping quarters, a kitchen, a parade ground, a theatre, a sick room and other common features, including workshops, were all contained within a secure perimeter area. There was also a guard room and cells. One of the peculiar features of the camp was a whole area that was set aside for high ranking German officers.

This was to be a camp that would house some of the more famous, or infamous, German prisoners of war. This would, of course, include high-ranking members of the German armed forces, including General von Rundstedt and his son. The General had been born in 1875 in Hanover and by September 1944 was Commander-in-Chief of all German units in the west. He had been captured with his son on 1st May, 1945. Von Rundstedt's experience of prison life in Britain was not typical, as he was considered to be an important prisoner of war. He was initially held at Wilton Park in Buckinghamshire and then transferred to Grizedale Hall. He arrived at Island Farm on 9th January, 1946. He was shuffled around for some time, undergoing interrogation, until he was finally transferred out of Island Farm in March 1947. The other feature of the Island Farm site, in the immediate aftermath of the escape from Camp 198, was that it was to be designated as a special camp, known as Special Camp 11.

The camp was transformed into a different sort of camp which would only hold senior German officers. Some of them were under suspicion of war crimes; others had already been charged with war crimes and were awaiting trial. There was another group that had either done deals with the Allies and were witnesses against other defendants, or had been cleared of any crimes but would still stand as witnesses in trials. There was also a group that were being held whilst extradition proceedings were underway for them to stand trial abroad.

Special Camp 11 officially came into existence on 17th November, 1945; however it was not until 6th January, 1946 that the first of the new batch of prisoners began to arrive. Amongst these was von Rundstedt. As a special camp, there was a much stricter regime. Although the men were held under the terms of the Geneva Convention, conditions were spartan at best.

Over the post-war years, the camp has shrunk and the remnants have been reduced to Hut 9, which was the hut from which the original tunnel was dug. In 2003, nearly 60 years after the escape attempt, the tunnel itself was reopened. It was found to be in an incredibly well-preserved state. There have been numerous articles written about the Island Farm complex and there have also been arguments in the press regarding the value of retaining this historic site. The site is fortunate that it has the Island Farm Heritage Group dedicated to not only protecting but restoring Hut 9 and, perhaps, to opening it as a tourist attraction in the future.

### Abbey Road Camp
Camp 284, which was listed as a German working camp, was Abbey Road Camp at Neath.

### Swanbridge Camp
Also listed as Camp 284 is the camp at Swanbridge, Sully.

Hut 9 Island Farm Prisoner of War camp, Bridgend. This is the hut that the German soldiers escaped from and is the only part of the former camp that has not been demolished. [*Image courtesy of Nigel Davis http://www.geograph.org.uk.*]

### Penclawdd

Penclawdd, Swansea was the location of Camp 408. Although the exact location of this site is unclear, there were two army camps in the St Mary's Hill area. One was a tented camp with a capacity of approximately 1,200 and the other a former US Army base for upwards of 700.

## Monmouthshire

### Claremont Camp

Camp 29 was a small prisoner of war camp in Claremont, Abergavenny.

### Mardy Camp

Camp 118 was Mardy Camp in Abergavenny. This camp first housed Italians and then became a German working camp. The campleader and German prisoners of war held a concert in Abergavenny Town Hall in February 1948.

### Llanmartin Camp

This site in Magor was designated as Camp 184. The base camp was initially used for the detention of all German ranks but, by 1947, it was being used exclusively to house German officers. This camp, like several prisoner of war camps in Britain, produced its own newsletter. The site finally closed towards the end of 1947 and is now a housing estate.

### The Mount Camp

Camp 197 was at The Mount Camp in Chepstow. The camp had been requisitioned early in the war and was the home of British and American troops for a number of years before the site became a prisoner of war camp. The Italian and later German prisoners were predominantly housed in Nissen huts.

### Llanover Park Camp

This site near Abergavenny was designated Camp 200. Having formerly been used as a US base camp prior to the D-Day landings, the camp was transformed into a prisoner of war camp for Italians and Germans. The prisoners worked on local farms. Many of the officers held at this camp were subsequently transferred to the officer-only camp (from 1946 onwards) at Camp 184 in Magor.

### New Inn Camp
Camp 677 was at Pontypool was designated as Camp 677.

## Montgomeryshire

### Glandulas Camp
Camp 101 near Newton housed Italian, German and Polish prisoners of war. The camp had a capacity of 850 prisoners.

## Pembrokeshire

### Haverfordwest
This was the home of Camp 199. The prisoner of war camp occupied the grounds of the former US army camp here and had a capacity of around 500 men. This site was also used as a Polish resettlement camp around 1947.

## Radnorshire

### Greenfield Farm
Camp 48 was at Greenfield Farm in Presteigne. The camp housed Italian prisoners of war from 1942 with most working on local farms. This tented camp was situated on a hill overlooking the small village of Presteigne, although huts were later constructed in the camp. The Italians remained in the camp for four years and were repatriated in 1946, sailing to Italy via Southampton.

### Pendre Camp
The site at Builth Wells was designated as Camp 573. This was an Italian prisoner of war camp.

# THE CHANNEL ISLANDS

## Guernsey

### *Castel Camp*

This site in Guernsey was designated as Camp 801. This prisoner of war camp operated as a base camp for just a year, between May 1945 and May 1946. Guernsey was liberated on 9th May, 1945, the initial inmates of the prisoner of war camp were, in fact, the former German garrison. Guernsey was in a deplorable state, as they had been cut off from supply routes in France since August 1944.

## Jersey

### *Fort Regent*

This camp in Jersey was designated as Camp 802. The base camp also only operated for a year, from 9th May, 1945, the first prisoners being the German garrison. In the First World War, a prisoner of war camp capable of holding 1,000 prisoners was constructed on Jersey, at Les Blanches Banques. The Germans had used Fort Regent as an ordnance depot and a labour camp. The fort was built between 1806 and 1814. Following liberation, the German garrison was then imprisoned in Fort Regent before being transported elsewhere. The fort remained in British government hands until 1958 when it was sold back to the States of Jersey. It has now been developed into a leisure centre.

## The Isle of Man

The Isle of Man's first arrivals were families of German origin. Towards the end of 1940, there were upwards of 14,000 German nationals who had been interned on the island. The Mooragh internment camp at Ramsey was sectioned off to separate the pro- and anti-Nazi individuals.

The Isle of Man had been used as a base for civilian internment camps in the First World War and, in fact, an entire self-contained camp had been created at Knockaloe. This was originally intended to house just 5,000 prisoners but, in the end, there were over 24,000.

During the Second World War, hotels were requisitioned and used as individual camps.

### Isle of Man Camp

The Mereside Empire Terrace in Douglas was designated as Camp 171, the Isle of Man Camp. The prisoners of war were held in the numerous bed and breakfast establishments and hotels in the area.

### RAF Jurby

There was a camp designated as Camp 702 at RAF Jurby. The RAF airfield had been opened in 1939 and was in the north of the island. Part of the airfield still remains and is used for airshows whilst the former prisoner of war camp is now the site of a new prison on the Isle of Man.

The Second World War RAF Control Tower at Jurby airfield has been preserved and is still used for its original purpose for air shows. [*Image courtesy of Jon Wornham http://www.geograph.org.uk.*]

# Chapter Four

# Escapes

WITH the prisoner of war camps filling up with die-hard Nazis and German, fortunes during the war remained buoyant until at least 1943. It is amazing that so few Germans actually tried to escape from imprisonment. However, there were attempts, and successful ones at that.

It is said that the only successful German escapee was one Oberleutnant Gunther Pluschow and he had escaped from Donington Hall in Derbyshire in 1915. His story is an incredible one of luck, sheer nerve and determination. Pluschow posed as a Dutchman and managed to make his way to Tilbury Docks and get aboard a steamer. When he arrived in Holland, he bluffed his way past the authorities and clambered aboard a train bound for Germany. He was awarded the Iron Cross for his actions.

For many years, the honour of being the only German prisoner of war to escape fell to Franz von Werra, but strictly speaking von Werra did not actually escape from Britain at all. Certainly he had tried, but he was recaptured and his actual escape took place en route to a prisoner of war camp in Canada.

## Island Farm, March 1945

Undoubtedly the biggest and boldest attempt to escape was launched as late as March 1945. There is continuing dispute about the actual numbers of German prisoners involved in the breakout. The estimates range from 67–84 although the exact number may never be known.

The Island Farm prisoner of war camp, designated Camp 198, was situated near Bridgend in South Wales. By comparison with many of the former prisoner of war camp sites, it is very well preserved. The story of the camp is very similar to many of the camps that were set up towards the end of the war. What is also significant about the camp was that later on in the war it became a special camp and housed a number of notable German prisoners who were awaiting the proceedings to begin at the Nuremberg Trials.

The camp had originally been constructed to house workers at the huge munitions factory in Bridgend. It was a disaster from the beginning with many of the (predominantly) female workers finding the place bleak and uninviting and preferring to commute from home rather than stay there. The place was mothballed until 1943 when it was used for the United States Army troops arriving in Britain in ever increasing numbers. As the men were deployed into Europe for the liberation of France in the summer of 1944, it was logical to seek a new purpose for the camp. The typical fate of many sites such as these was to be turned from army camps into prison camps. The entire infrastructure was in place and the overall layout of the camp was perfect for conversion into a prisoner of war camp.

Nonetheless, by the time the first German prisoners of war began arriving, the conversion had not been completed. The prisoners themselves were pressed into creating their own camp and were involved in converting the concrete huts and putting up the barbed wire fences. The camp was given the number 198 and was originally designed to hold as many as 2,000 Italian and German prisoners. After some changes, it was decided that the camp would only hold German officers. The first of the officers began to arrive in November 1944.

From the outset, the German officers were determined to escape. They began to dig two tunnels. The first of them was discovered in January 1945, the other remained operational. The Germans planned their mass escape for 10th March, 1945. They had created a tunnel no less than 21m long from Hut 9 out beyond the perimeter fence. The tunnelling could not have been easy as the camp was situated in an area that has a heavy clay soil.

The Germans used a variety of different tunnelling tools from tin cans to knives stolen from the canteen. The soil from the tunnel was scattered over the prisoners' garden plots and other places around the camp. The Germans had also constructed a false wall in one of the huts and rolled the clay up into pellets and pushed them through a hole into the void.

They cannibalised anything they could find to shore up the tunnel, including parts of bed legs and oak benches. They even managed to assemble a ventilation system underground with a Heath Robinson contraption made of tin cans. The Germans had also rigged up lighting for the tunnel by running a cable from the main camp supply.

It was an audacious escape attempt, well planned and executed. The escapees were organised into small groups, each group had a compass and map. Identity papers had been forged and food supplies had been collected.

The first of the escapees wriggled through the tunnel at around 2200 on the night of 10th March, 1945. One group managed to steal a car and drive as far as Birmingham. Another group was picked up in Southampton.

The exact numbers of escapees may never be known. One theory is that 84 actually got out of Camp 198 and that 14 of these were captured very quickly. This allowed the official figure of escapees to be brought down to 70. However, this was later amended to 67 as it is rumoured that three of the men got as far as Kent and were never seen again. What became of these men is unknown.

There was a tremendous uproar about the escape. It was even suggested that either a spy or an anti-Nazi in the camp had thrown a note over the wire with full details of the escape plan but nothing had been done. The camp was certainly undermanned as far as guards were concerned and the regime there had become too relaxed. It is important to bear in mind that at the time the Allies were on the brink of crossing the Rhine and marching into Germany and that the end of the war in Europe was only two months away.

In the immediate aftermath of the escape and recapture of the German prisoners, the whole camp was broken up and the remaining 1600 Germans were transferred to other facilities. Island Farm was re-designated as Special Camp 11. It then became a holding centre for 160 high ranking German prisoners of war awaiting screening, who would eventually face trial in Nuremberg for war crimes. The camp was finally closed down in 1948 by which time all of the prisoners had been returned to Germany. The question about the so-called Canterbury Three, the three Germans spotted in Kent after the escape has never been truly resolved or explained. Perhaps they did make it back to Germany?

### Camp 13, November 1941

Although the Island Farm escape attempt in March 1945 was the largest and the most audacious of all of the escape attempts from Britain, it was by no means the first. Two German Luftwaffe pilots were being held at Camp 13 (Shap Fells Hotel) at Penrith in Westmorland. Oberleutnant Harry Wappler had been on a bombing mission on 13th September, 1940. Wappler's target was Ellesmere Port, which they bombed, but on their return journey back to their base near Paris, they ran into barrage balloons set up by the 966th Barrage Balloon Squadron near Newport.

Wappler's Heinkel bomber hit one of the balloon cables at a height of around 2,000m. The aircraft was damaged but managed to continue flying until it hit a second cable. The aircraft crashed into a house, killing two of household. Wappler managed to bail out, but the other three crew members were killed. Wappler was captured and sent to Camp 13. Here he met Leutnant Heinz Schnabel. He had been a Messerschmitt pilot flying the Me109 fighter. Schnabel had been escorting some German Dornier 17 bombers with other members of his squadron on a raid against Croydon on 5th September, 1940. Schnabel was heading back to base after the attack when the formation came under attack from the RAF. His aircraft was shot up and he was forced to land near Aldington in Kent.

Wappler and Schnabel hatched a plan to escape from Camp 13. On a foggy Sunday, 23rd November, 1941 the two men hid in a wood pile inside the camp until nightfall. Using a pair of pliers they had made, they managed to open the perimeter wire enough to squeeze out and make off towards the nearby railway line. They clambered aboard a train heading for Carlisle.

The escape must have been well organised as the men had flying jackets on over their uniforms and identity cards which claimed that they were Dutch pilots. Once they got to Carlisle, they managed to bluff their way into RAF Kingstown, which was then being used by No 15 Elementary Flying School. An air apprentice, Alan Gaydon, helped start up a Miles Magister training aircraft for them and they climbed aboard and took off, heading south.

They had not got very far when it became clear that the aircraft was low on fuel. With amazing bravado, they landed at another RAF airfield and managed to persuade the RAF crew to refuel for them. They took off again with the intention of making for German-occupied Holland. They quickly realised that the aircraft did not have the range for the journey across the North Sea and turned back for the British coast.

Wappler and Schnabel landed some five miles north of Great Yarmouth. Still pretending to be Dutch, they were taken to the RAF airfield at Horsham St Faith. Their luck ran out, however, as the theft of the aircraft had now been reported and they were arrested. The pair were given a month's solitary confinement and then sent to Canada for the duration of the war.

## Escape and murder

The German Military Cemetery at Cannock Chase in Staffordshire has the graves of two German prisoners of war. One was an officer and the other was a sergeant major. They were both murdered by fellow German prisoners of war at Camp 21, Cultybraggan Camp near the village of Comrie in West Perthshire.

The murder of Sergeant Major Wolfgang Rosterg actually has its roots at Camp 23, the Le Marchant Barracks at Devizes in Wiltshire. Rosterg was believed to have been the son of a German industrialist. He was in his early 30s and had operated as the camp interpreter at Devizes.

Devizes had been used as one of the camps to handle the particularly hardcore Nazi German prisoners. It was here that their political views were screened before they were passed on to other,

Cannock Chase Military Cemetery is the main graveyard for First and Second World War German and Austrian dead in Britain. The 5,000 graves include those who died in prisoner of war camps and were transferred from their original burial plots around the UK when the cemetery was established in 1967. [*Image courtesy of Colin Smith http://www.geograph.org.uk.*]

more secure camps. As a result there were thousands of particularly strong-willed, unrepentant Nazis at Devizes. They had come up with an incredible plan. Not only did they intend to escape, but they also had decided that they would steal vehicles and equipment and march on London. They would release other German prisoners of war and the incredible plan was that they were to be supported by German paratroops.

It seems that the idea was to coordinate the incredible escape around Christmas of 1944. This would coincide with the last great German offensive in the west in the Ardennes. Consequently, the date set for the audacious escape attempt would be 16th December, 1944.

It was not, however, a great surprise to the British. Bletchley Park, the centre that intercepted and decrypted German signals, had picked up several messages relating to the plan. There was also talk in the camp, which was picked up on by the guards and, of course, there were informers. It also appears that Devizes camp had a number of hidden microphones.

It will probably never be known whether Rosterg was recruited as a British spy. But as a known anti-Nazi it was either unfortunate for him or a deliberate attempt to install an informer, that Rosterg was one of the men that was transferred out of Devizes to Cultybraggan on 17th December, 1944. He was transported to the new camp by bus. The camp was guarded by Polish guards. Rosterg was one of 30 or so other prisoners that had been transferred that day. They went through initial screening, where their identification papers and numbers were checked; they had a physical examination and were then assigned to their barrack blocks. Rosterg must have stood out, as he was assigned to Hut 4 in Compound B, with 80 other much younger fanatical Nazis.

Just two days after Rosterg arrived at the camp, the body of Major Willi Thornan was found. Three days later Rosterg's body was found.

Rosterg was able to read English and the prisoners were allowed to read British newspapers. It would have fallen on Rosterg to translate the news stories to an expectant audience that were certain that the German attack in the Ardennes would be a turning point in the war. The Nazis did not believe a word of any of the stories, which firmly suggested that the attack was doomed.

For whatever reason, the Nazis placed some of the blame both for their transfer and for the passing on of propaganda to Rosterg. A court martial, or *Ehrenrat*, was convened in the hut. The Nazis were certain that either Rosterg was a defeatist, an anti-Nazi or a British spy. It would appear that the questioning was brutal to say the least. He was beaten with iron bars that had been heated on the stove. His body showed evidence of innumerable injuries; he had been kicked, punched and it is believed that his head had been smashed into kerbstones in front of the barracks.

Rosterg's body was found at 0900 on 23rd December, 1944 by the Polish guards. The official cause of death was strangulation. It would, however, appear that he had been beaten virtually senseless, dragged into the latrines where a rope was wrapped around his neck and he was then hauled up and hanged from a water pipe. Rosterg would not have been able to even call out for help as he had been gagged.

Initial investigations met with a conspiratorial silence. The only comment made was that Rosterg had been thrown into a lion's den and that he had simply been in the wrong place at the wrong time with the wrong people.

The British authorities were determined to get to the bottom of the matter and John Wheatley was brought in to investigate. Wheatley would later become a life peer as Baron Wheatley and was the Lord Justice Clerk. At the time he was serving with the Judge Advocate General's Branch. This was an organisation that was responsible for court martial processes in the armed forces. Wheatley could immediately see that the camp was volatile.

Helping Wheatley was a German Jewish interpreter, Herbert Sulzbach. Sulzbach had managed to escape from Germany in the 1930s and had fled to Britain. He was one of the many Germans and Italians that were rounded up shortly after the outbreak of the Second World War and put into an internment camp on the Isle of Man. Subsequently he joined the Pioneer Corps. It was his linguistic skills that brought attention and he was used across Britain working in interrogation centres.

The initial investigations of Wheatley and Sulzbach revealed that Rosterg had been translating newspaper articles to a stunned and disbelieving audience. There were calls for him to stop translating the propaganda but he continued. There was an argument and apparently Rosterg told them that he was not a filthy Nazi like the rest of them. This was the final straw and a German court martial of sorts began, which led to his murder.

At the end of the investigation eight prisoners were charged with murder. The eldest was only 21. They were removed from the camp and put into confinement in London. The trial opened on 10th July, 1945, at Kensington Palace gardens, in front of a military

Pentonville Prison where five German prisoners of war were hanged for murdering a fellow prisoner. [Image from the *Illustrated London News*, 1842.]

tribunal. One of the eight men agreed to give evidence against the others and was acquitted. Another was acquitted of the murder, but the remaining six were found guilty. Five of them were hanged at Pentonville Prison on 6th October, 1945. The sixth man had his death penalty commuted and he spent eight years in prison.

The first of the murderers was one of the ring leaders of the plot at Devizes. He was a former German paratrooper, Erich Pallme-Koenig. There were three SS men, Joachim Goltz, Heinz Brueling and Kurt Zuchlsdorff. The final man was from the German navy, Joseph Mertens. The sentence was carried out by the famous British hangman, Albert Pierrepoint, with the executions being carried out at half hour intervals.

Pierrepoint also executed two other Germans who had been found guilty of beating Gerhardt Rettig to death. This murder also seems to have had its roots in the Devizes escape attempt. The two men were Armin Kuehne and Emil Schmittendorf. The murder apparently took place on 24th March, 1945 in a prisoner of war camp near Sheffield.

The camp where Rettig's murder took place was Lodge Moor Camp (Camp 17). It may have been that there was a new escape attempt in the offing and that Rettig was accused of having given away the escape plan. As it was, he was chased around the camp by a number of other prisoners and was caught and beaten. The prison guards managed to get him out and take him to hospital, but he died from his injuries. Schmittendorf and Kuehne were two of four men that would face trial. The other two were Heinz Ditzler and Juergen Kersting. In actual fact both Schmittendorf and Ditzler, just two days after the killing of Rettig, crawled under the wire at the camp and managed to escape. They were only at liberty for a short period of time, however, as they were quickly recaptured. At the trial, Ditzler and Kersting were acquitted due to lack of evidence.

### Fog is their friend

The British constantly complain about weather conditions, yet thick fog and poor visibility are certainly a would-be escapee's best friends. There are two fog-based escape attempts in Staffordshire, although they may in fact be precisely the same escape that is attributed to two different camps.

At Camp 194 at Penkridge in Staffordshire, 13 prisoners of war, under cover of heavy fog, cut through the wire. The men split up but two were picked up in Wolverhampton, two in Derby and another two in Walsall. Another two men were apparently picked up in Liverpool.

An extremely quick-witted policeman managed to scoop up four of the escaped prisoners of war. The men had stolen a car and then run out of petrol. The policeman told them that he could take them to someone who would give them a lift to the nearest petrol station. In fact he boldly marched them into a police cell.

As to what became of the 13th man, nothing is recorded. He was with the two men that had been picked up in Liverpool. It was their intention to try to stow aboard a neutral ship. The 13th man was never returned to Camp 194, so whether he actually managed to get away or was simply sent elsewhere may never be known.

Close to Camp 194 was Camp 96, on Wolseley Road in Rugeley. As soon as it became apparent that the 13 Germans had escaped there was jubilation, followed by a determined attempt to rush the main prison gate as the Germans armed themselves with shovels or anything else they could lay their hands on. A calm and collected Camp Commandant refused to budge and threatened to shoot any man dead who came near the gate. The Germans' bravado ebbed and they returned to their huts.

## Massive Italian escape

The escape attempt from the Doonfoot Camp in Ayrshire (Camp 14/112) was so huge that it even makes the Island Farm escape attempt pale into insignificance. Once again this was a tunnelled effort to escape.

The escape took place in December 1944 and incredibly 97 Italians were involved in the plot. Within a relatively short period of time 93 of them were recaptured by camp guards. But four were still at large.

There were three naval officers, Corini, Gianoli and Foglia and an Italian soldier, Pirisinu. Technically speaking the four men, as far as the Scottish police force is concerned, are still at large because nobody ever told them that the escapees had been rounded up by the camp guards and put back under lock and key.

There was a sad postscript as far as this camp is concerned. Apparently an unnamed Italian prisoner of war committed suicide in early 1945. He was a motor mechanic, was anti-Fascist and deplored the fall of Italy but had come to love the British. He was clearly suffering from depression.

## Back in Staffordshire

The German prisoners of war in Camp 194 were not finished with their plotting and planning. Some time after the escape of 13 men under cover of fog, another, even more elaborate, plan seems to have developed, this time involving a tunnel.

The tunnel's entrance was under a bed in Hut 4 and the idea was to tunnel out of the camp. It would be a mass escape attempt involving over 100 men. The camp guards thought something was going on, but try as they may their searches revealed no sign of a tunnel. The tension in the camp was palpable and it was the German camp choirmaster that cracked first. Terrified that the escape attempt and tunnel would be discovered, he decided to confess. Dumbfounded, the other camp inmates saw him striding towards the camp gate to inform the guards. Belatedly they gave chase, but he managed to slip through the gate and give the game away. For his own safety he was transferred to another camp.

## Dog tags

At Camp 176, Glen Mill near Oldham in Lancashire, the camp administration had set up a system that appeared to be a foolproof way of ensuring that they knew how many prisoners of war were using the sports ground. A guard was placed in a hut at the entrance to the sports ground. Any prisoner of war wishing to use the sports ground had to hand in his identity tag. In effect this meant that the British would know exactly how many and who was on the sports ground at any given time.

The Germans hatched a plan. There was an opportunity for men to hide in a hole under a mound of earth near the construction site of a tennis court. One of the British guards was convinced to allow one of the prisoners of war to help him collect the tags. The prisoner of war stood hard up against the window, through which the tags had to be passed to the guard. This blocked the guard's view of the men passing the hut.

The helpful prisoner then called on his colleagues to pass their tags forward so that he could give them to the guard. Four men slipped past, out of the view of the guard. The would-be escapees hid in the hole under the pile of earth until darkness. They emerged and cut the wire around the sports ground, then slipped away. They were quickly rounded up and after an investigation the British camp guard was sentenced to three months imprisonment for neglect of duty.

This was not the only escape attempt from Camp 176. The German senior officer, Lagerfuehrer Schaffer, had his own office. Inside the office were cigarettes and rations that were dolled out to the prisoners of war. Schaffer was persuaded to allow a tunnel to be dug from his office, using large crates to shield the entrance.

The German conspirators were perhaps not as clever as they had hoped. Camp authorities were suspicious when all of a sudden there was a huge leap in demand for replacement light bulbs. Knowing something was up, the Camp Commandant issued the order that he would only allow the issue of a new light bulb on presentation of a broken one. Already some additional light bulbs had been dolled out and of course these were destined for the tunnel.

It seems that the Germans in this camp were also singularly unlucky. Working in the dark and confined environment of the tunnel, one of the escapees swung his pick and managed to burst the water main that connected the prison to the main town supply.

The men working in the tunnel were now in a quandary. The tunnel was fast filling with water. The options were stark; they could drown or they could risk electrocution when the water reached the rudimentary electrical wiring, or they could attempt to get out and reveal the location of the tunnel. They chose the latter, which was probably just as well.

Faulty measurement and engineering had meant that the tunnel was actually not heading for cover, where they had intended it to emerge, but it had reached a road. Had they continued to tunnel, the first truck that passed over would have collapsed the whole thing and buried them under thousands of tons of soil.

## Accidental death

The German prisoners in Camp 176 were a busy lot. There was yet another escape attempt when seven of the men cut through the perimeter wire and made off into the countryside. They were all recaptured, but as soon as the escape attempt was known, the Camp Commandant ordered a roll call. The Germans had chosen a good time to escape; it was pelting with rain and visibility was poor. The Germans assembling for the roll call were understandably rowdy and rather jubilant. They were also not that keen on getting soaked to the skin.

Because there had been an escape, additional camp guards were drafted in to try to take control of the situation and later to take part in the search for the escapees. One of the guards who was actually assigned to an anti-aircraft gun, stood nervously as the Germans refused to line up to be counted. He fired a shot in warning, but instead of the bullet whistling over the heads of the cavorting German prisoners, it smacked into the face of an 18-year-old prisoner of war, Paul Hartmann.

Hartmann was killed instantly and his body was buried in the cemetery close to the camp. There was an inquest held in secret, which must have exonerated the camp guard, as he continued to work at the camp. Even the Germans must have known that it was an unfortunate accident, as no vengeance was ever sought against him.

As for the seven escaped prisoners of war, two of them were picked up in Wakefield, one at the railway station in Castleton and four in Leeds. They had managed to get 30 miles away before being recaptured.

### The Marauder escape

What is believed to be the last attempt by Germans to steal an Allied aircraft and get home to Germany, took place in December 1944. The attempt was made from Camp 180, at Marbury Hall in Cheshire. Marbury Hall at the time was being used as a camp where captured enemy prisoners were sorted before being sent on to other camps. They had already been partially sorted at Camp 9, on Kempton Park racecourse.

Unfortunately, not much is known about the escape attempt, but the escapees were four German air force officers. Close to Marbury Hall was the USAAF air base at Warrington. Somehow the four Germans slipped through the Marbury Hall perimeter fence and made their way onto the American base. Not only that, but they also clambered onboard a B26 Marauder. When they were discovered by an American Military Policeman they were fiddling with the controls, trying to work out how the aircraft worked.

There were undoubtedly hundreds more attempted escapes and dozens of instances where German or Italian prisoners of war managed to elude capture for short periods of time. It is interesting

---

**A dramatic escape abroad**

Even German and Italian prisoners of war who were shipped out to Canada or the United States still attempted to escape. There was the story of the Italian prisoner of war, Felice Benuzzi, and two other prisoners, Giovanni Balletto and Enzo Barsotti, who escaped from Camp 354 in January 1943. Incredibly, this camp was in Kenya. The story of the escape is brilliantly told by Benuzzi himself in his own book, *No Picnic on Mount Kenya*. The film, *The Ascent* (1994) was based on the real events.

The three Italians escaped in January 1943, and using only improvised equipment and whatever rations they had set aside they actually climbed Mount Kenya and were absent for 18 days. What is even more remarkable about the whole thing is that at the end of their adventure they actually broke back into the camp and gave themselves up. This must rank as being one of the most incredible and perplexing Axis escapes of the Second World War. The Italians would need to have escaped to neutral Portuguese East Africa, a thousand miles away and across a dangerous landscape, with no money and no ability to communicate with locals. They had no map, but still managed to reach the summit. They had reached nearly 5000m, just short of the highest part of the mountain. At this point they made their descent, turned themselves in at the camp, enjoyed their first hot meal in days and were then put into solitary confinement.

---

to note that these prisoner of war escapes by German, Italian or other Axis Allies have never really captured the imagination. This is in stark contrast to the legendary stories of The Great Escape, Colditz or the wooden horse. This is not to say that the Axis escapes were in any way less dramatic, or less desperate.

# Chapter Five

# The Bonzos

THERE was another way of escaping detention. But just like tunnelling under a wire or cutting through it and then facing the prospect of traversing a hostile country to gain freedom, the alternative was equally as hazardous.

Amongst the thousands of Axis prisoners of war were many that would willingly cooperate with the Allies. This was not just to secure their freedom. Some were undoubtedly genuine anti-Nazis. Others had come to the conclusion that as the Russians inexorably moved west, overwhelming German forces, there was a distinct possibility that Germany would be lost forever. The alternative, of course, was to work along with the Western Allies to bring the war to a more favourable conclusion.

The men that were recruited were codenamed Bonzos. They were passed on to the British Special Operations Executive (SOE). The SOE had been created in July 1940 with the idea being that it would carry out guerrilla warfare and lend aid to local resistance movements in Axis occupied countries. It was a brainchild of Sir Winston Churchill, who charged SOE with setting Europe ablaze.

SOE grew to become a huge organisation. By the end of the war it was directly employing 13,000 people and around a third of these were women. Throughout the course of the war SOE could claim to indirectly control around a million resistance fighters and partisans.

It had been a long-held belief that an ideal situation would be to support any anti-Nazi underground in Germany and Austria.

Lieutenant Colonel Ronald Thornley ran the German and Austrian section. The trouble was that there was no real German resistance, so any agents sent into Germany or Austria would find it impossible to survive as there was no established network in place. Experience in other occupied countries showed that a complex network of agents and friends were required for the operatives to move to safe houses and be able to make regular communication by radio. As a consequence, agents that SOE had tried to get into Germany were picked up pretty quickly.

The idea then changed to trying to create the illusion of an anti-Nazi movement that was planning a coup against Hitler and the German government. This was codenamed Periwig and it was launched in November 1944. Carefully, SOE began fabricating evidence that a combination of the German army, the Nazi Party, the police force, industrialists, the Roman Catholic Church, foreign labourers and other groups were all conspiring to overthrow Hitler.

The subsequent use of German prisoners of war could be considered to be rather cynical. The men were not told that their mission into Germany was in fact a sham. Withholding information from the German volunteers revealed another level of deception. The German volunteers were told that they had been trained and were to be infiltrated into Germany in order to make contact with a resistance movement that did not exist. If, or rather when, these prisoners of war were captured they would undoubtedly be interrogated by the German authorities. No matter what torture was used, they would ultimately attest to the fact that everything they had been told by the British pointed toward a real resistance movement. SOE went to the trouble of sending radio equipment, weapons, supplies and food onto imaginary drop zones, certain in the knowledge that the Germans would pick up these supplies and mistakenly believe that they were intended for resistance fighters. SOE broadcast fake wireless traffic and they also broadcast, via the BBC, German code phrases just as they had done in French prior to the landings in Normandy in June 1944. SOE was also active in passing on false information to double agents. No German traveller in a neutral country was safe either;

SOE agents would intercept their luggage and insert fake but incriminating documents.

It actually proved to be slightly more difficult to find Bonzos than the SOE had originally anticipated. It is believed that around 50 of them were ultimately recruited and it does seem that they were not exactly high grade agents. But for the SOE purposes this did not matter.

Two Bonzos were dropped by parachute near Bremen on the night of 2nd to 3rd April, 1945. One of the men, Gerhardt Bienecke, was to pass on codes and signals to an SS officer in Berlin. The other man, Leonhardt Kick, was to link up with an imaginary resistance cell in Bremen. Both men tried to carry out their missions and in fact Kick, who had documents claiming that his name was Kauffmann, shot a Gestapo man who challenged him. After this he headed towards Delmenhorst, near Hamburg and turned himself in to Allied troops as a British agent.

Bienecke, who was using documents naming him Breuer, had certainly tried to carry out his mission and the next that was heard of him was in August 1945 when he told Russian troops that he was in fact a British agent.

Two more Bonzos were also parachuted into Germany in April 1945. They were told to make for the Bavarian mountains and contact a resistance group based there. They were to train the resistance fighters in handling parachute drops of troops and supplies. The two men, Otto Heinrich (or Hoffmann) and Franz Lengnick (or Lange) both survived and later confirmed that they had in fact contacted anti-Nazis and had tried to carry out sabotage missions.

Other German prisoners of war were used for different purposes, which presumably gave them access to either improved conditions or better rations. The Political Warfare Executive Propaganda Section Head was behind the plan to send letters from German prisoners of war in Britain addressed to others in Canada or the United States to Germany instead. They were sent in such a way as to suggest an accidental misdirection. Inside the letters would be hints about an organised German resistance.

There were a number of German prisoners of war that actually went through the process of being screened by Section X of the SOE. Initially they were interrogated at a camp on Boxhill Road in Dorking, Surrey. Those that passed the initial screening were sent to genuine SOE training schools. They were kept separate from the other trainees. The men also received parachute training at Ringway airfield. A holding school for the men was set up at Wanborough Manor, Puttenham near Guildford. It would appear that 51 German prisoners of war were trained, and some 28 of them were actually sent on active missions. Seven men were specifically trained at Gardeners End, Ardeley near Stevenage in Hertfordshire as part of the Periwig Operation.

### Lieutenant Colonel Ronald Thornley
Lieutenant Colonel Ronald Thornley had worked as a businessman in Europe before the war. His knowledge of Germany was almost unrivalled and he could speak the language fluently. He had entered military service in 1939 and had come top of his staff training course for the SOE at Brickendonbury Manor. He would go on to lead Section X until November 1944.

Thornley was also involved in other operations that used captured Germans. Perhaps one of the most famous and controversial was the Foxley Operation. This was a plan to assassinate Hitler. It is believed that the assassination attempt was due to have taken place either on 13th or 14th July, 1944, when Hitler visited the Berghof, which was his home in the Bavarian Alps. The plan was to send in a Polish German speaker by parachute, along with a British sniper. The sniper would use a standard German army rifle. The link with prisoners of war was that a German prisoner, Dieser, had an uncle living in the area. There are various reasons put forward for the operation not going ahead. On the one hand Hitler was doing such a poor job of directing the German war effort that whoever replaced him would certainly be far more effective. The second reason is that there were concerns that Hitler would be considered a martyr. As it was, Hitler made his last visit to the Berghof in July 1944 and he never returned.

Thornley was also involved in the XX or Double X system. The idea was to turn captured German agents, or in fact create fake agents, which could pass information back to the Germans in order to deceive them. The British had been extremely effective and indeed fortunate in scooping up the vast majority of German agents that had been sent to the British Isles. Some had simply turned themselves in but others, as a result of their poor training, had been captured. The Germans had tried to take advantage of the fact that huge numbers of refugees were trying to make their way to Britain during the war years. This method of sending fake refugees via neutral countries was the most commonly used German method. Others had been sent in by parachute or dropped off by submarine. According to post-war records every single German agent that had been sent to Britain had either been captured or had given themselves up. There may be one exception to this and that was an individual who committed suicide. These agents were kept 'on ice' and effectively MI5 ran the entire German espionage system in the UK. They provided their German handlers with detailed information about markings on vehicles; they sent copies of stolen documents and false reports on successful bombing missions by the German air force. One of the most successful deception plans worked perfectly when these German agents provided overwhelming evidence that the bulk of Allied forces were in fact poised to land at Calais rather than Normandy. The Germans were so convinced by the information that they initially discounted Normandy as a diversionary attack and no less than 15 divisions were kept at Calais as a result.

**Trent Park**
One of the centres of operations was Trent Park, which was the Combined Detailed Interrogation Centre. This is now part of Middlesex University. It was initially used to interrogate German U-boat personnel. Another important location for turning German prisoners and agents was the London Cage. This was run by MI19, who also ran Trent Park.

Interrogation was an important part of the process that enemy prisoners of war went through. The London Cage had five interrogation rooms and a capacity of 60 prisoners. Although officially not endorsed by the British authorities and in breach of the Geneva Convention, there were accusations that torture was undertaken here. The London centre was run by Alexander Scotland, who vigorously denied that any torture was ever used.

The centre was later used to house and interrogate German war criminals, including those who were implicated in the murder of 50 Allied prisoners of war that had escaped from Stalag Luft III some 100 miles to the southeast of Berlin. This is the famous 'Great Escape', which took place on the night of 24th to 25th March, 1944. Around 600 Allied prisoners of war were involved in the construction of the tunnels. Seventy-six men escaped, of whom 73 were recaptured. All three of the successful escapees were RAF pilots: two Norwegians and a Dutchman. Fifty of the recaptured Allied prisoners of war were executed. Some 18 Germans implicated in the massacre were held at the London Cage and faced trial in 1947.

German prisoners of war in Trent Park, 1943. [*Image courtesy of the German Federal Archive.*]

**Italian prisoners of war**

Certainly in the aftermath of the Italian surrender in 1943, the overthrow of Mussolini and the realignment of Italy as part of the Allied cause saw huge changes in the treatment and trust of Italian prisoners of war. In fact many of the men who had been in prisoner of war camps since 1940 had already proven themselves to be largely trustworthy and disinclined to cause trouble or to escape. There were, however, notable causes for concern. Perhaps the most famous and dramatic took place at 11.11 on 27th November, 1944.

Seven years previous, the Air Ministry had bought a disused Gypsum workings near the village of Fauld in Staffordshire. It became RAF Fauld, an underground munitions storage depot. Working there were considerable numbers of Italian prisoners of war. In fact 194 of them were working in the old mines at the time of the accident. Naturally sabotage was a possibility. An explosion occurred, detonating some 3,670 tons of bombs and ammunition. Fauld was the site of the largest explosion in the UK. Only three larger blasts ever took place during the course of the whole of the Second World War and these were all nuclear explosions. The result of the explosion can be seen to this day, as the crater covers 12 acres and is up to 90 feet deep. An entire reservoir containing around six million gallons of water disappeared. The rescue work took three months. Around 78 people were killed. On the nearby memorial a number of Italian names are clearly visible. The probable cause is now thought not to have been sabotage but possibly an accident caused by the inexperience of some of the Italian prisoners of war. In 1974 the cause of the explosion was finally released. The suggestion was that one of the Italians had removed a detonator with a brass chisel rather than a wooden batten and that this had caused the first explosion and then the subsequent second explosion.

A prime example of the obvious comparisons between Italian and German prisoners of war is the experience and attitude of those that were shipped to the United States. In the period June 1940 to May 1943 the Allies took some 600,000 Italian prisoners of war. Fifty-one thousand of these were subsequently shipped to the United States. When Italy signed an armistice on 8th September,

1943, Mussolini was still alive and supported by the Germans in Northern Italy. Nonetheless, some 90 per cent of all of the Italian prisoners of war in the United States joined Italian service units. They worked on industrial and farming sites across the USA. Those that refused to cooperate were kept in a number of camps under strict security in states such as Arizona, Hawaii, Texas and Wyoming. In effect the Italians that had joined the service units now had jobs and pay. They could mix with other Italians or those of Italian descent. The Italians in the USA were repatriated in January 1946. The American government was strict in terms of immigration and if any of the Italians wished to marry American nationals they had to do it in Italy and then wait for their opportunity to return to the United States. There are no official figures suggesting how many Italians did in fact marry Americans and then began new lives in America.

In the UK a considerable number of Italian prisoners of war and an estimated 25,000 Germans chose to stay in Britain after the war. As we will see, they forged new lives for themselves. It was clear that those that had had the opportunity to mix with the British population had developed a strong affinity to the British way of life.

# Chapter Six

# Staying On or Going Home

ON 14TH August, 1947, there was a marriage at the Civic Centre in Southampton. Normally this type of event would have been unlikely to have even been featured in the local newspapers. But this was a marriage with a difference, as it was the first British woman to marry a German prisoner of war. It had only just been allowed by government legislation, and so was the first of its kind. The couple, Heinz and June, would be featured on the front page of newspapers across the world. In 2007 they celebrated their 60th wedding anniversary. The result of their wedding was six children, 12 grandchildren and 15 great-grandchildren.

Heinz Fellbrich had been captured in 1945 and was eventually sent to Camp 402, or Camp C19, in Southampton. June Tull had been working in a nearby bottling plant. Heinz, meanwhile, was working on building prefabricated homes in the area. They had been incredibly fortunate to meet, since Heinz had been captured by the Americans in Alsace. He was shipped out to Boston and then held in a prisoner of war camp in Pennsylvania. Around a year later he was shipped to Britain.

At the time of their marriage the couple received a huge amount of hate mail, in fact two sacks full. They had also been confronted by people who would spit at them and punch them. June was considered a traitor. It had been a very difficult courtship, as Heinz was required to return to the prisoner of war camp at dusk, even on his rest days, and was expected to always wear his prisoner of war uniform. This meant that he was barred from visiting pubs or the cinema. It seems that June's father aided and abetted the courtship, as on some occasions he lent Heinz his suit. Even on their marriage night Heinz was expected to return to his camp. Heinz was released in February 1948 and settled in the Eastleigh area.

In fact the British government, by June 1948, was becoming rather concerned about the number of Germans that had remained in Britain after the war. Under the codename Operation Repat the Home Secretary was to sign deportation orders for 10,000 of the 25,000 Germans who had settled in Britain. There were plans to ship the Germans to hostels that would be guarded by the police. Any that refused to leave would be sent to Chelmsford prison. The men would be shipped out via Harwich beginning in November 1948. Troops would be on standby in order to prevent any serious demonstrations.

Germany was in a state of chaos in the post-war years. Literally millions of people were on the move. The estimate has been put at

German prisoners of war under British guard. [*Image courtesy of W. Wolny.*]

anything between 12 and 14 million. Some of Germany had been handed over to Poland, the Soviet Union and to Czechoslovakia. These countries expelled Germans from the area, displacing millions. Many Germans had fled west as the Soviet army had swept across Poland and into Germany during 1944 to 1945.

For some of the German prisoners of war, their homes in Germany were now gone. For even greater numbers their homes were now in the Soviet occupation zone of Germany. Few had much to go back to and those that did risked being rounded up and deported to labour camps in Russia. In any case, returning to a war torn Germany would mean extreme hardship. Even in West Germany there were massive housing shortages until the 1960s and unemployment was high.

Perceptions about marrying former enemy nationals certainly changed over time. A prime example is that of a Scot who had seen service as a member of the British Army in Germany during the Second World War. The eventual result was David McAllister, who is now the Prime Minister of the German state of Lower Saxony. David was born in 1971, some seven years after his parents, a Scot and a German national, were allowed to marry. He was brought up in West Berlin. David McAllister is tipped to be a major force in German politics in the future.

There are countless stories of German and Italian prisoners of war settling in Britain or marrying British women. Perhaps the most famous is the former Manchester City goalkeeper Bert Trautmann, who was awarded the OBE in 2004.

**Bert Trautmann**
Trautmann had been born in Bremen in 1923 and was an apprentice motor mechanic when war broke out in 1939. He joined the Luftwaffe and went on to become a Fallschirmjäger, or paratrooper. Trautmann was stationed in Poland and a practical joke involving a car resulted in injury to a sergeant, which led to his being court-martialled and sentenced to three months in prison; his first taste of camp life. Trautmann went on to serve on the Eastern Front, winning a number of medals for gallantry, including the Iron Cross. By the time he was posted to Normandy he had been promoted to

the rank of sergeant. He was eventually captured by the Americans and found himself being transferred to a prisoner of war camp in Britain. He was moved around, spending time at Marbury Hall in Cheshire, and then Camp 50 near St Helens in Lancashire. It was here that he remained until 1948.

Trautmann played quite a lot of football during his time as a prisoner of war, but as an outfield player. When the camp was due to close, Trautmann decided to stay on in Britain and work on a farm, then help out with bomb disposal in Liverpool. He was also playing amateur football.

Manchester City offered Trautmann a contract in October 1949. Some 40,000 supporters marched the streets of Manchester to protest about the signing of Trautmann and season ticket holders threatened to boycott the club's games. Nonetheless, after his first appearance in November 1949, Manchester City supporters began to warm to him. He still received massive abuse, which he blamed as the reason for letting in seven goals against Derby County in the following month. But soon he established himself as one of the best goalkeepers in Britain.

Incredibly, in the 1956 FA Cup Final, Trautmann was involved in a collision with a Birmingham player. What Trautmann did not know at the time was that he had actually broken his neck. He played on and Manchester City won the game. Trautmann took several months to convalesce. He ended his career in 1964, having played 545 matches for the club.

Trautmann married Margaret Friar and he had three children with her. Eventually Trautmann had been completely accepted by Manchester City fans and the British public. He had even stated that he supported England even if they were playing against Germany.

### Happy marriages
There were huge numbers of other marriages between British women and either Germans or Italians during the war and here are a few prime examples:

Margaret Stratton married German prisoner of war Peter Roth in Peterborough on 22nd May, 1948. They encountered an entirely different reaction to that of Heinz and June. Hundreds of people lined the streets to witness their wedding day. Peter was from a village near Frankfurt and had been captured in Normandy in 1944. Margaret, when she first saw him was smitten, and on the day they met, Peter raided his prisoner of war camp's garden of every flower he could find to give to her. She returned the compliment by giving him a cigarette and a piece of cake. At the time, fraternisation was forbidden but the couple contrived to spend Christmas Day together in 1945. Margaret paid a local taxi driver to bring Peter from the camp 13 miles away. Someone had told the local police, but Margaret was so well-known and respected in the community that they decided to allow it to happen.

Franz Kamp married Pat Goodall shortly after the war. Franz had been captured in August 1944, after spending three years fighting on the Eastern Front. He was fortunate enough to have been captured by the Americans in France. He was sent to Italy and then transported to America, but brought back to Europe to a prisoner of war camp in 1946. The couple would go on to have five children. Franz had worked at several farms in Yorkshire before meeting Pat.

There is also a story of a marriage in the Devizes area of Wiltshire. In 1950 Yvonne Trevorrow married the German prisoner of war Hans Bittner. Yvonne was working on a farm in Marston. The Germans were being held at the Le Marchant Barracks, and there were also Italians held at Devizes Castle. Yvonne was a frequent visitor to the swimming pool in Devizes and it was there that she met Hans. He was being held at Patney, which was a small prisoner of war camp offshoot. Hans was working as the interpreter there. Yvonne managed to contrive a transfer to a farm closer to Patney. Their love affair blossomed, but over the period 1947 to 1948 the Germans were being repatriated. Hans was in fact repatriated to Bavaria. They wrote to one another and as fortune would have it, Yvonne's father was in the British Army in Kiel. She went to visit him for three weeks in the summer of 1948 and Hans came up to stay with them for three days. Yvonne's father initially was set against their marriage. But eventually he came round to the idea and helped with the paperwork. Finally permission was granted and the only proviso was that Hans married within the next six months. They did indeed marry at St Mary's Church in February 1950, although Hans still had to report to the police every week.

### The Italian job

It was not just Germans that married in Britain and remained there after the war. This story of an Italian who married a Sardinian rather than a British woman clearly loved England so much that he returned to Somerset with his new wife after the war to settle. John Salvatore Zuncheddu was born in 1920 in Sardinia. He joined the Italian army and was taken prisoner near Tobruk. Initially he was sent to Alexandria and then to Johannesburg in South Africa. He and his comrades were now split up; some were shipped to Britain whilst others would cross the Atlantic to the United States or Canada. John arrived in Liverpool in July 1941 and was transported to Acton. After screening he was sent to Camp 44 near Bridgwater in Somerset, where they were housed in Nissen huts. After a few weeks John was considered one of the prisoners trustworthy enough to leave the camp each day to carry out agricultural work. In time they actually slept on farms rather than returning to camp each night. In any case they wore brown uniforms with yellow flashes so they could easily be spotted if they strayed.

In 1945 the Italian prisoners were assembled at Wookey Hole. Before being taken there John had had a conversation with Edward Moxey, for whom he had been working for some months. Moxey had asked him whether he would like to come back to work for him on a permanent basis. John had agreed and after 18 months back home in Sardinia he returned to Somerset, leaving only once more to marry Rosetta on 15th April, 1950. John died in Somerset on 15th April, 2010.

### Multiple marriages

There are certain areas of the country that have close associations with multiple marriages, one of which is the Henllan Bridge Farm prisoner of war camp in Carmarthenshire in Wales. The camp was fairly standard, with 35 huts, a theatre, a hospital, a kitchen and other facilities. The first inmates were Italian prisoners of war that had been rounded up in North Africa. They arrived in May 1943 and many of the locals watched them being marched from the train station through Henllan to the camp; initially there were around 1,200 of them. They all worked on local farms. In 1946 some 700 of the men were repatriated to Italy, but some chose to stay in the local area and many of them settled down and married in Wales.

Henllan Camp is, of course, well known for the chapel that Italian prisoners of war made. Mario Ferlito did most of the painting. The chapel is still used for masses, particularly on Remembrance Sunday, with many people from the Italian-Welsh community in attendance.

In Scotland too there is thought to be around 30,000 Scottish Italians as a result of Italian settlement in the First and Second World Wars. There are several well-known personalities that belong to the Italian-Scots community, including Tom Conti and the comedian Armando Iannucci.

## Not always a happy ending

Sometimes, the relationships between prisoners of war and British women would end in disaster. In August 1947 a 22-year-old German prisoner of war was given a year's hard labour for attempting to run away with his 16-year-old British girlfriend. Shortly afterwards, two German prisoners did indeed escape with their girlfriends. They were recaptured in Thurso. Somehow they managed to get away again and disappeared, probably never to be recaptured. One girl even tried to commit suicide after her mother refused to allow her to marry her German boyfriend. Luckily, she was found by the boyfriend and taken to hospital after swallowing tablets. A death did occur in Middlesex when a former German prisoner of war was shot by his girlfriend's father.

Prior to July 1947 it was illegal for prisoners of war to have relationships with British women. In fact in early 1947 Werner Vetter was given 12 months imprisonment after his affair with a British woman came to light. Legally if a British woman married a

German prisoner of war she lost her British nationality. She also had no right to live with her husband whilst he remained under military supervision. The marriage would not stop the prisoner of war from being repatriated, but the law did stop at forcibly deporting the wife.

## Changing times

Under the new rulings, which effectively came into force in 1948, the government took a more sympathetic view. In fact prisoners of war that married British women had far more freedom and they had a right to stay in Britain provided they had a job. Some newspapers reacted very badly to the change in the law and predicted a rush by Germans to get married to avoid being repatriated. Up until 1948, around 800 Germans married British women during their period of internment, and after that time there were certainly many more marriages.

As the regime switched, from incarceration in the prisoner of war camp, with little opportunity to mix with British civilians, to a freer system of internment rather than imprisonment, relationships developed. Prisoners were able to adapt and learn English. Some of the prisoners became such an integral part of the farms they had worked on that some were actually given pieces of land from the farmer. Others inherited the whole farm from childless owners and, of course, others married the farmer's daughter. Some of the prisoners, even after they had been released and returned to Germany, made trips back to the farms so that they could help out with the harvests.

For many of the prisoners, Germany presented an unknown. Many of them, even after they were permitted to return, wanted to stay a little longer in Britain. Inevitably, those that chose this course ended up staying either for many more years or for the rest of their lives. Some of the Germans in particular had no idea where their families had been relocated after 1945. Their homes were gone and in many cases their entire families had been wiped out.

Some of the Germans went on so-called release holidays, where they visited Germany and saw for themselves the desperate situation there, particularly in the east. There was also the problem for Germans that had been members of military units that they were identified by the Russians as essentially war criminals. The inevitability for them of a return to the east would mean relocation far further east, probably in Siberia.

Any new friendships or love interests for Germans or Italians often brought moral dilemmas. Some, of course, already had girlfriends or indeed wives at home. There were certainly instances of bigamy either intentional or unintentional.

For prisoners of war that were quartered on farms, all that was necessary to ensure that they stayed in Britain was for the farmer to fill out an application form at the County War Agricultural Executive Committee office. This was a system that was set up in

Sicilian prisoners of war, en route to their homes. [*Image courtesy of The Library of Congress Prints and Photographs Division, no. 8d34147u.*]

May 1947. In order to obtain residency in Britain there had to be a first stage of temporary residency, which lasted until the end of 1948. After that the prisoner was likely to receive an unrestricted permit or leave to remain.

Each of the Germans still in prisoner of war camps went through a selection process, some of which evaluated their political attitudes, but largely their value as a member of the workforce.

In terms of numbers, it is difficult to know precisely how many Italians stayed, but there are broader figures for Germans. According to government statistics there were some 23,729 classed as civilian workers in Britain in September 1948. Just over 19,500 of these men were in England or Wales; over 11,000 were living on farms. In Scotland there were just over 4,000 and around half of these were living on farms. There were still 120 prisoner of war camps and hostels operational across the country. This was the period in which the second phase of the residency selection took place. In order for them to qualify they had to commit to working in agriculture and have a contract with a farmer. Although this would appear to be restrictive and not wholly attractive as a proposition, there were still far more applicants than places. Each regional office handling the former prisoners tried to match applicants with suitable work. Some had to pass on the names of individuals to neighbouring areas in order to help them find a contract with a farmer.

Operation Repat took place at the end of November. The idea was to transport those who wanted to go home or those who had not managed to get themselves a contract. Eleven vessels left Harwich between 23rd November and 13th December, 1948. The Germans were taken to the Hook of Holland and then onto Munster, where they were released. Although it was a relatively successful operation, nearly 300 Germans turned up too late to be repatriated using this system. In fact there were 50 who were supposed to have been repatriated but were still in hiding by March 1949.

Again, in terms of repatriation and those that stayed, it is the German figures that are complete. In line with the Geneva Convention, these German workers were entitled to take a month's leave in Germany. Confusingly this was run at the same time as the repatriation. Nearly 8,400 chose to go on leave to Germany between the middle of December 1948 and middle of February 1949. By the following month around a thousand had opted to remain in Germany and not return to Britain. This meant that by the end of the leave period an unreliable figure of 15,649 German civilian workers were in Britain without restricted residency.

For those with German wives or girlfriends there was a difficult conundrum. If the German soldier had become a British citizen prior to 31st December, 1948 the wife automatically became a British citizen, regardless of where the marriage had taken place. After this date German wives had to apply to the Home Office.

The contribution of Italian and German prisoners of war to the British economy and productivity cannot be underestimated. Successive waves of British male volunteers, conscriptions and moves to other forms of work had had a drastic impact on British agriculture. The use of prisoners of war in the early stages of the war was fairly limited, but by 1943 the British reliance on school children and the Women's Land Army had begun to be offset by the use of prisoners of war. The number of prisoners of war working on the land in 1941 was pretty small and almost exclusively Italian. By the time the war had ended it was mainly Germans working on the land. In fact, that figure peaked at 170,000 in March 1947. German prisoners of war represented nearly two per cent of the British workforce at that time.

In the immediate post-war period up to 60 per cent of all prisoners of war remaining in Britain were working on the land. Although figures are hotly disputed, it is believed that around 150,000 Italians and nearly 390,000 Germans worked in some capacity or another during the war period and its immediate aftermath.

As we have seen, a large number of Germans did remain as civilian rural workers after the repatriation phases in 1948. This figure is probably around 15,700 men. The Italians, on the other hand, were given their choice to either cooperate or not cooperate in September 1943. Those that did cooperate, could earn a decent wage and were not placed under the same kind of strict security that those who chose not to cooperate were subjected to. It has been estimated that only around 1,400 Italians were rural workers by 1944.

## From prisoners to willing workers

Most of the prisoners of war, certainly during the war years, were not quite as productive as regular civilian workers. This is partly due to the fact that their wages were quite low and that their willingness to work ebbed and flowed with the fortunes of their country on the battlefield. By the end of the war those that had been working on the farms had become very proficient. They were also less hostile and irresponsible and, in fact, local populations were far more accepting of them and realised their value. According to a document produced for the British Cabinet in September 1945, there were severe concerns about encouraging the repatriation of Italian prisoners, as many of these were highly experienced milkers and farmers whose absence would be felt in terms of productivity. Statistics compiled for that secret document of September 1945 indicate that 62,000 Italians were working on the land out of a total of 154,500. By this time, they had been overtaken in terms of numbers by the Germans, of whom just over 101,000 were working on the land.

As late as 1945, the British government was keen to hang on to at least 30,000 Italians, as their work on farms and in general agriculture was so valuable. Politically, the sooner the Italians were repatriated the better, but economically it was worth offering them pay to stay on. Some of them had become indispensible and it was those that were particularly skilled in farm work that would be amongst the first eligible for repatriation. This was because they had fully cooperated and not misbehaved.

There was no real way around the problem; the bulk of the Italians would have to be repatriated and their places on farms taken by Germans. There were plans afoot to actually move Germans in prisoner of war camps on mainland Europe to Britain to undertake heavy unskilled labour in Britain. It was estimated that in September 1945, for example, there were 225,000 German prisoners on the Continent. Of these it was reckoned that 163,000 were suitable for employment. However at the time there were already 400,000 German prisoners in Britain. It was also reckoned that of that number, 20,000 of them were diehard Nazis and for various other reasons around 13,000 more were not suitable for employment.

The decision seems to have been taken that these men, that for one reason or another were not productive, should be removed from Britain as soon as possible and be replaced with men that would work. It was proposed that German prisoners would work on road building, housing sites, railways, harbours and docks, in the public utilities, in land reclamation and drainage and on coastal defence work. The target number of workers from the camps was suggested to be 200,000 and it was decided that this workforce could be achieved by around June 1946.

The Russians, of course, used German and Italian prisoners of war for hard labour too, but this was not the view of the Americans. The Americans did not propose to employ prisoners of war as forced labourers. They were in fact pressurising Britain to accelerate their demobilisation so that the need for forced labour would disappear. However, many Germans in particular would remain in Britain until at least the end of 1947, when an estimated 250,000 prisoners were repatriated. Some remained for virtually another year, when the last repatriations took place in November 1948. It has also been estimated that around 24,000 chose to stay on in Britain. Some of these had come to love Britain; others knew that their homes had disappeared and there were also those that intended to marry British women and start a new life in Britain.

# Chapter Seven

# The Legacy of the Camps and Prisoners

THE SECOND World War prisoner of war camp period can be broadly dated as 1941 to 1948. Across the whole of the British Isles there were approximately 340 main camps and around 1,200 smaller facilities, such as hostels. Significantly, the bulk of the prisoners in the period up to 1943 were Italians. From September 1944 in particular the balance shifted and month-by-month tens of thousands of German prisoners of war were held in Britain. The probable peak was September 1946, when over 402,000 German prisoners of war were still being held in Britain.

Understandably, given the fact that some months saw as many as 40,000 prisoners arriving in Britain, the camps were often 'make do' facilities, or hastily purpose-built. This is why we see such a wide range of different buildings being used as a centre for camps. Before the end of 1942 the vast majority of them were buildings already in existence, such as mills, schools, race courses and country homes. By the end of 1942 some of the new camps being established were purpose-built, however, given the speed at which they were needed and the lack of manpower and resources, they tended to be made from materials that were not designed to last any great length of time. This meant that most of the buildings were from prefabricated concrete, in sections, with corrugated iron roofs. Some were built on essentially Greenfield sites, whilst others were built on sites that were no longer needed by the Allied armed forces, such as airfields or former army camps.

In April 1995 the National Lottery funded a major survey of military sites in Britain. Initially, former prisoner of war camps were not included in the survey, but their cause was taken up by English Heritage and this led to a report being published in 2003, which identified most of the sites and for the first time gave them a classification based on what was left of the site in the present day. Undoubtedly there were many sites that had been entirely removed. There were others where there were just partial remains. The survey, however, found that five purpose-built camps were virtually complete and seven more had considerable remains.

These can still, of course, be seen today. There is Moorby Camp in Lincolnshire, Harperley Camp in County Durham, St Martin's Camp at Gobowen in Shropshire, and the two Yorkshire camps, Eden and Thirkleby. One is now a light industrial estate, two are parts of farms, one is a national museum and the fifth, Harperley, attained the status of an ancient monument in 2002. It is worth looking at Harperley in a little more detail, because this has had a chequered history.

Harperley, or Camp 93, closed as a prisoner of war camp in 1948 and was used after that to house displaced persons, mainly those from Eastern Europe. During the war, having been built by Italian prisoners in 1943, it was set up to hold around 1,400. It was also the headquarters camp for most of County Durham and there were satellite camps in a number of locations in the immediate area. The buildings primarily had brick or concrete foundations. There were around 50 of them and the roofs were made from corrugated asbestos sheeting. Arguably it is the best preserved of all of the prisoner of war camps in Britain, as it has the full range of all the different buildings, including the guard compound, the parade ground, canteen, theatre and remnants of the fencing.

The camp itself was purchased by private owners in 2001. They tried to sell it in 2009 in the hope that it would attract an investor who could return the camp to its former state. The owners, however, received a grant from English Heritage in 2011 to carry out vital work as a result of the harsh winter. The prisoner of war camp hit the headlines in September 2009 when the owners tried to sell it on eBay. They had been forced to close the shops and café

Harperley Camp was decorated by some of the prisoners of war with murals based on memories of home. [*Image courtesy of Rolyat29.*]

on the site when they had run out of money. The owners had already spent upwards of a million on refurbishments. The long-term future of the Harperley Camp is still not guaranteed, although with its protected status there may be hope for it.

The Harperley Camp was due to be demolished back in the late 1990s to make way for a business park, but fortunately the camp has, for the time being, been saved. It is still possible to see some extraordinary and well preserved murals that were painted by the German prisoners, some of whom remained there for as long as five years.

It was Italian prisoners, however, that really made their prisoner of war camps home from home. Back in 1942 a prisoner of war camp was built near the village of Henllan in mid-Wales. It was designed to hold around 1,000 prisoners. The Italians that were held there, the first of which probably arrived in May 1943, were prisoners of war from Libya and Tunisia. The 1,200 men had made a long and arduous journey. They had been shipped from North

Africa and then to Glasgow. They were then held under guard for their train journey via Derby and Gloucester to the prisoner of war camp. The majority of the prisoners worked on local farms but they soon made the camp a little piece of Italy, with their own opera company, band and football teams. One thing, however, was still missing, and that was a Roman Catholic Church.

The British Commandant allowed the men to convert an empty hut into a Catholic church. The prisoners used all sorts of scrap, including old bully beef tins, to make the pillars and candlesticks. The altar was made from concrete and off-cuts of wood. The most exceptional part of the creation was the mural and fresco, which

Churchill Barrier No 2, near St Mary's, Orkney. The Churchill Barriers were formally opened by the first Lord of the Admiralty on 12th May, 1945 – just in time for the war's end. As a result, their lasting role was not as a defence for Scapa Flow, but as a series of causeways linking the five islands together. The other lasting legacy of the building of the barriers came from the employment there of over 1,300 Italian prisoners of war, captured in North Africa. It is usually forgotten that 800 of these men were housed in camps on Burray. Much better known are the 550 who were housed in Camp 60, on the northern slopes of Lamb Holm and who used spare material to build the chapel there. [*Image courtesy of Nicholas Mutton http://www.geograph.org.uk.*]

was painted by Mario Ferlito. He made his own paint from fruit, vegetables and tea leaves and, incredibly, the murals are still as bright and fresh today as they were when they were first painted. The creation, known as The Church of the Sacred Heart, is believed to be the only one of its type in Britain.

This is only true as far as the mainland is concerned, because there is another called The Church of the Barriers. This is located in the Orkneys. Again, Italian prisoners of war built the structure. The camp was on Lamb Holm and called Camp 60. It was the home to 550 Italian prisoners of war who had been shipped to the northern most reaches of the British Isles in order to take part in the construction of four permanent barriers, which linked a chain of islands from the mainland of Orkney to South Ronaldsay.

In fact, there were several Italian prisoner of war camps in this area, including some 800 on Burray. The causeways are incredible. The four causeways or barriers collectively are around two miles long and the prisoners dropped huge wire cages into the sea to create the foundations. Some 40,000 cubic metres of rock were dropped into the sea and the visible part of the barriers consists of approximately 300,000 tons of concrete blocks.

The Italian chapel, along with a nearby statue of St George, is all that remains of the camp on Lamb Holm. Originally there were 13 huts but the Italians were keen to improve the camp and the statue of St George was designed and made by Domenico Chiocchetti. It is made from barbed wire covered in concrete.

Towards the end of 1943 the camp padre, Father Giacombazzi, and the Commandant, Major T P Buckland, came to an agreement that a chapel could be constructed. Two Nissen huts were fitted together with the original idea that one half would be a chapel and the other half a school. Work began towards the end of 1943. Chiocchetti took charge of construction. The eastern end was lined with plasterboard, an altar was made from concrete, and two windows were painted. The prisoners pooled their funds to buy curtains for either side of the altar. Chiocchetti began painting the interior whilst a second prisoner, Palumbo, who was an iron worker, began work on the rood screen.

The altar art of the Italian chapel and Lamb Holm, Orkney. The bricks have been painted onto the interior of the Nissen huts. [*Image courtesy of Des Colhoun http://www.geograph.org.uk.*]

The prisoners quickly came to the decision that the whole of the two Nissen huts should be turned into a chapel and improved. Some of the plasterwork was painted to look like brickwork. Other prisoners began work on the outside, building an ornate facade and they also built a belfry and created a moulded plaque to place above the door.

Sadly, the chapel was not entirely finished before the Italians were repatriated in 1945. Chiocchetti remained behind to finish off the font and the locals promised to look after the chapel. Over 10 years later, a committee was set up to ensure the preservation of the chapel. Chiocchetti returned in 1960 to help restore some of the paintwork, and he also returned a second time to make further improvements. In 1992, 50 former prisoners came back to Lamb Holm but, unfortunately, Chiocchetti was by this time unwell. He died in 1999.

Images found on the chapel roof to the left of the altar, painted by the Italian prisoner of war, Domenico Chiocchetti in the chapel at Lamb Holm, Orkney. [*Image courtesy of Des Colhoun http://www.geograph.org.uk.*]

Arguably the most famous of the prisoner of war camps is the Island Farm site near Bridgend in South Wales. It was, after all, the location of the biggest and most audacious escape attempt by German prisoners of war during the Second World War. Unfortunately, however, very little remains of the camp itself. The bulk of the camp was demolished in the early 1990s and the rubble was originally supposed to be used to help extend a runway at Cardiff airport. All that now remains of any significance on the site is Hut 9.

Some of the former German inmates at Island Farm made a return to the camp in 1976. The long-term future of the remaining hut on the site hangs in the balance, although supporters hope that it will eventually become a museum and visitor centre. A number of photographs, paintings and artefacts belonging to the camp's prisoners have been discovered at the site.

In order to see one of the most complete prisoner of war camps still in existence a visit to Malton in North Yorkshire is necessary. The Eden Camp is as complete and unchanged as it was when it was finally closed as a prisoner of war camp in early 1949. The original site was requisitioned in early 1942 with tents, so the permanent camp was not built until 1943. The Italian prisoners of war only spent a short time there, until it was used by Polish troops being prepared for operations on mainland Europe. German troops stayed there from the middle of 1944 to the beginning of 1949. It was then used for the next five years as an agricultural holiday camp.

The site was then used to store grain and rear pheasants. By the 1970s some of the huts were sublet as workshops. A company then bought it in the mid-1980s with a view to set up a factory on the site. As luck would have it, some Italian ex-prisoners of war visited the site in 1985 and suggested that it should be opened as a museum.

In March 1987 their wish came true when the museum initially opened using 10 of the 33 huts. Over the next decade, after winning several tourism awards, successive huts were opened up with displays of artefacts and information about many different aspects of warfare.

There are still large numbers of former prisoner of war camp sites that retain some clues as to their former use. This is particularly true of the camps that were former army barracks or RAF airfields. Clearly there are also a large number of country houses and other historical properties that were once the centres of tented prisoner of war camps. Sites that have returned to private hands tend to have the majority of their prison camp heritage erased, although aerial photographs will betray the footprints of Nissen huts, the lines of pathways and vestiges of perimeter fences.

Whilst the physical remains of the prisoner of war camps can be seen in most counties and areas up and down the British Isles, the undeniable link between those that were imprisoned and the country in which they were forced to live, sometimes for many years, has remained strong.

Incredibly, in 2009, there was a fascinating story linking a former SS soldier and a remote part of Perthshire in Scotland. Heinrich Steinmeyer was a member of the 12th SS Panzer Division. He was involved in the vicious fighting around Caen in 1944 and his division, which comprised former Hitler Youth, fought a fanatical resistance against British and Canadian forces. By the time the division was finally overrun, only 12 remained of Steinmeyer's unit. As an SS man he was designated as a 'black prisoner'. Ultimately he was shipped to the Cultybraggan prisoner of war camp in Perthshire, Scotland (Camp 21). Although he was not to know it at the time, he would spend the next seven years there.

Steinmeyer was amazed with the kindness that was shown to him and the fact that they were well looked after medically and well fed. He was one of those men whose home in Eastern Germany had been handed over to Poland. In time, the inmates were allowed to carry out building work in the local area, and others worked on farm. Steinmeyer worked as a farmhand. He was amazed that the locals would often give him money in order to buy essentials. Some of the locals even sent food parcels to his family after he explained to them that they were living in abject poverty.

Eventually, after living in Stranraer for some time building a dam, Steinmeyer went home to Germany and became a dock worker in Bremen. He visited Scotland in 1988 and since then has returned on a regular basis. In 2009 he announced that as he had no children or close relatives himself he intended to leave his estimated fortune of £430,000 to elderly residents living in the village of Comrie and the town of Stranraer.

The Cultybraggan Camp is one of the best preserved prisoner of war camps in Britain. It was originally constructed in September 1941. There is some confusion as to whether it ever actually held any Italians, but we do know that by May 1944 just short of 800 German prisoners of war were there. It was originally designated as a transit camp and could hold up to 4,500. It was later re-designated as a base camp for 'black prisoners' and was a high security camp. It was closed down in May 1947 but continued to be used as a military training camp until 2004. According to the Buildings At Risk Register for Scotland it is categorised as being 'at risk'. The site consists of a number of Nissen huts, and planning permission has been granted to develop the site for businesses and garden allotments. There are also plans to set up a local history project on the site.

Whilst Steinmeyer still retained his love of Scotland but returned to Germany, another German prisoner of war in Scotland experienced an entirely different set of circumstances.

In October 2010 Heinz Roestel was reunited with his sister Edith after being apart for 80 years. Heinz had been in the German army and was captured in Holland and sent to a prisoner of war camp in Scotland. He had already lost touch with his younger sister, as they had been separated when their mother had died. Heinz was one of the many Germans that chose to stay on in Britain after the Second World War, largely on account of the fact that his hometown of Hindenburg was now part of southern Poland. What he did not know was that his sister was looking for him and in the summer of 2010 she tracked him down to Penpont, a small village in Dumfries and Galloway.

Before Edith came to Scotland, Heinz suffered from a stroke, so Edith found him in hospital. He still recognised his sister who had only been six years old when he had last seen her. Heinz had been held at the Carronbridge Camp, where he had worked on local farms. He eventually married a Scottish girl and settled in the area.

Heinz had become so British that he actually had forgotten the bulk of his German and had to use an interpreter to communicate with his sister.

Heinz is not the only German in the Dumfries and Galloway area to have permanently settled there. Another, Richard Michalek, was captured by the Americans in Normandy in 1944. Initially he was shipped to Britain but then made the long Atlantic crossing to the United States, where he worked in cotton fields in Oklahoma. Eventually he made his return to Britain and chose to stay on in Scotland after the war. Richard kept his German passport.

It does seem incredible that even when Britain stood alone until the end of 1941, facilities and resources had been set aside to house enemy prisoners of war. Some Italian and later German prisoners of war were of course shipped to farther flung reaches of the Empire. Some 37,000 for example were transported to remote camps in Canada.

The first batch of German officers was sent to Canada in June 1940. In fact Canada had been taking German seamen from England since September 1939. There were also prisoner of war camps in Australia. Although it might be expected that Australia would house Japanese prisoners of war, incredibly large numbers of Italian and German prisoners were shipped there initially from the Middle East and North Africa. The Australian government had been warned that they might have to accommodate upwards of 50,000 prisoners.

As in Canada, there are a number of sites that still exist in Australia, where prisoner of war camps can still be seen. An ideal example is the Cowra site, which is due west of Sydney. This camp held Italians, Japanese and Koreans. As far as the Germans were concerned, it is believed that the first German prisoners of war to arrive in Western Australia were over 300 from the vessel *Kormoran*, which was sunk in November 1941. The first Italians to arrive in Western Australia appeared in the middle of 1942. The Italian prisoner peak population for Western Australia alone was 3,500 by February 1945.

Although the enemy prisoners of war were undoubtedly frustrated and disappointed with their capture, it would appear that their treatment in Britain was far more lenient than Allied prisoners who found themselves in the numerous German prisoner of war camps. Life in the British camps was tolerable. The more diehard Nazis were not trusted and, on occasion, rightly so. The vast majority could, however, look forward to work outside the camp and a degree of freedom.

The surrender sheets promised the Germans safe conduct if they surrendered and became prisoners of war.

It is surprising that given the numbers involved, so little is known about the unwanted guests that spent years in the British Isles during and immediately after the Second World War. Some sites, such as Eden, Harperley, Island Farm and other locations are all that now remains of a vast network across the whole of the British Isles.

There is still an interest in the escapes from German prisoner of war camp, and films, dramas and documentaries constantly appear. Yet so little is known and even less has been written about the experiences of the enemy prisoners of war and the uncertainty of returning home, even after the war had ended. So little now remains and what does remain is fragile. Without careful preservation even this part of our country's history may disappear forever.

# Bibliography

**Books**

Hellen, J.A., *Temporary Settlements and Transient Populations. The Legacy of Britain's Prisoner of War Camps.* Archive for Scientific Geography 53 (3) 191–211 (1999).

Reid, P. and Michael, M., *Prisoner of War: The Inside Story of the POW from the Ancient World to Colditz and After.* Chancellor Press (2000).

Sullivan, M.B., *Thresholds of Peace. German Prisoners and the People of Britain 1944–1948.* Hamish Hamilton (1979).

Thomas, Roger, *Prisoner of War Camps (1939–1948).* National Monuments Record English Heritage (2003).

**Websites**

www.bbc.co.uk – Useful website, including memories from those imprisoned in the camps such as: http://www.bbc.co.uk/history/ww2peopleswar/stories/99/a2473599.shtml and http://www.bbc. co.uk/history/ww2peopleswar/stories/06/a5972006.shtml.

http://www.culturalprofiles.net/Scotland/Units/4444.html – Information about Inchdrewer House.

http://www.historic-scotland.gov.uk/index/heritage/historicandlistedbuildings/listedbuildingsresults.htm – Details of listed buildings, including prisoner of war Nissen huts in Scotland.

www.kg6gb.org/prisoner_of_war_mail.htm – Malcolm Sanders' great site on prisoner of war mail, with good listing of sites. Sadly, this is no longer a live site.

www.islandfarm.fsnet.co.uk – Brett Exton's site on the Bridgend escape with lots of useful information and links.

http://www.projectinspire.co.uk/ – Research project about Leeds prisoner of war camps.

http://www.quornmuseum.com/display.php?id=1014 – Details of the Quorn camp.

www.secretscotland.org.uk – Fascinating gazetteer of abandoned sites across Scotland.

http://www.shgc.uk.com/history.php – Details of the Shooters Hill prisoner of war camp which took over part of the golf course.

http://visit.carmarthenshire.gov.uk/did-you-know/henllan-POW-camp.html – Details of the Henllan Bridge Farm prisoner of war camp.

http://wartimegilford.com/powcamp/ – Details of prisoners of war in Portadown, Northern Ireland.

http://www.ww2talk.com/forum/prisoners-war/20535-italian-pow-uk-camp-59-botesdale-diss-norfolk.html – Details about some of the prisoner of war camps in Norfolk.

# Index

**Aberdeenshire**
Deer Park Camp 128
Stuartfield Camp 127–128
Tullos Hill 128–9

**Anglesey**
Camp 32 149

**Angus**
Kinnell Camp 129
Tealing Airfield 129

**Argyll**
Glenbranter Camp 129–130
Knapdale Camp 130

**Ayrshire**
Doonfoot Camp 130
Kingencleugh Camp 131
Maidens or Kirkoswald Camp 131
Pennylands Camp 130–131

Balletto, Giovanni 173

**Banffshire**
Duff House 131–132
Sandyhillock Camp 131

Barsotti, Enzo 173

**Bedfordshire**
Church Farm 32
Ducks Cross Camp 30
Harrold Hall 32
Luton Airport 31–32
Mansion Potton Camp 31
Old Woodbury Hall 32
Sutton Park 33
WD Camp 30–31

Benuzzi, Felice 173

**Berkshire**
Basildon House 34
Crookham Common Camp 35
Durnell's Farm Camp 35
Lodge Farm 33
Mortimer Camp 33
Stanbury House Camp 33–34
Winter Quarter Camp 33

**Berwickshire**
Ninewells Camp 132

Bevin, Ernest 136
Bienecke, Gerhardt 177
Bittner, Hans 187–188

*211*

**Borders**
Leet Water 132
Stobs Camp 132

**Breconshire**
Talgarth Hospital 149

British Special Operations Executive (SOE) 175–182
Brueling, Heinz 167

**Buckinghamshire**
Hartwell Dog Track Camp 36
Hitcham Park 37
Norduck Farm 36–37
Shalstone Camp 36
Wilton Park Camp 35–36

**Caernarvonshire**
Pablo Hall Camp 150

**Caithness**
Watten Camp 133

**Cambridgeshire**
Barton Field Camp 37–38
Friday Bridge 38
Histon Camp 39
Lower Hare Park 38
Sawtry Camp 38
Trumpington Camp 38
West Fen Militia Camp 39
Yaxley Farcet Militia Camp 39

**Carmarthenshire**
Abergwili (Glangwili) Hospital 151
Henllan Bridge Camp 150–151
Llanddarog Camp 151
Ystrad Camp 151

**Cheshire**
Boar's Head Camp 40
Crewe Hall 41–42
Dorfold Hall Camp 43

Dunham Park Camp 41
Knutsford 40
Madeley Tile Works Camp 42
Marbury Hall 40–41
Parkgate Camp 43
Racecourse Camp 40
Toft Hall Camp 39–40
WD Camp at Ledsham Hall 42

Combined Services Detailed Interrogation Centre (CSDIC) 23, 35, 179–180
Command Cages 25–26, 179–180

**Cornwall**
Consols Mine Camp 44
Pennygillam Farm Camp 43
Scarne Cross Camp 43
White Cross Camp 43

**County Antrim**
Lissanoure Camp 124

**County Armagh**
Elmfield Camp Gilford 125
Gosford Camp 124–125

**County Down**
Holywood Camp 125–126
Rockport Camp 124–125

**County Durham**
Blackbeck Camp 48
Coxhoe Hall Camp 48
Harperley 44–47
Oaklands 47
Walworth Castle 47–48
West Boldon Camp 48
Windlestone Hall Camp 44
Wolviston Hall 48

**County Tyrone**
Dungannon 126
Lisnelly 127
Monrush Camp 126

**Cumbria**
Beela River Camp 50–51
Grizedale Hall 49–50
Hornby Hall 51
Merry Thought Camp 50
Moota Camp 50
No 4 Camp 51
Shap Wells 50
Warwick Camp 52

**Denbighshire**
Pool Park Camp 151

**Derbyshire**
Alvaston Camp 53
Nether Heage Camp 52
New Drill Hall 52
No 1 Camp 53
Oaks Green 52
The Hayes 52
Weston Camp 53

**Devon**
Bampton Road Camp 54
Bickham Camp 53
Bradninch Camp 54
Bridestow Camp 55
Chaddlewood Camp 54, 55
Country House Hotel 55
Cruwys Morchard 56
Dymond's Farm 54
Exhibition Field Camp 53–54
Handy Cross Camp 56
Hazeldene Camp 54
Home Park Camp 55–56
Ivybridge Camp 56
Nisson (or Nissen) Camp 55
Winsford Towers Camp 54

Ditzler, Heinz 168

**Dorset**
Cattistock Camp 56–57
Merley Park Camp 57

Motcombe Park Camp 56
Park Camp 57

**Dumfriesshire**
Barony Camp 133
Carronbridge Camp 133–134
Dryffeholme Camp 134
Halmuir Farm Camp 133
Honduras Camp 134
Isles House Stables 134

**Dunbartonshire**
Blairvadach Camp 135
Stukenduff 135

**East Lothian**
Amisfield Camp 135
Gosford Camp 135–136

**Essex**
Ashford Camp 57–58
Bentley Farm 58–59
Berechurch Hall Camp 58
High Garrett Camp 57
Ickleton Grange 59
Mill Lane Camp 57
Purfleet Camp 59
Radwinter North Camp 58
Shaftesbury Camp 59
White House Camp 58

Fabian, Inspector Robert 110
Fellbrich, Heinz 183

**Fife**
Annsmuir Camp 136
Bonnytown Camp 136
Capeldrae, Westfield 136

**Flintshire**
The Ordnance Storage Depot 152

Gable, Clarke 114
Geneva Convention 16–17, 180

**Glamorganshire**
Abbey Road Camp 154
Island Farm Camp 152–154
Penclawdd 155
Swanbridge 154

**Gloucestershire**
Ashton Gate Camp 62
Bedminster Camp 62
Bourton Camp 62
Leckhampton Court Camp 63
Northway Camp 63
Northwick Park Hospital 62
Sedbury 61
Spring Hill 62–63
Sudeley Castle Camp 59–60
Wapley Camp 62
Wynols Hill 60–61

Goltz, Joachim 167

**Guernsey**
Castel Camp 157

Hague Convention 16–17

**Hampshire**
Anglesey House 63
Arena Road Camp 65
Beaumont Barracks 67–68
Carfax Estate 64
East Cams Camp 64
Fargo Camp 66
Fisher's Camp 64
Ganger Camp 63
Haig Lines 65
Hiltingbury Road 66
Oakhanger 66–67
Ossemsley Manor 65
Park House A 65
Puckridge Camp 66
Quarr House 65
Setley Plain Camp 64
Southampton Common 64

Stoneham Camp 64
Whitchurch Camp 66
Willems Barracks 67

Hartmann, Paul 172

**Herefordshire**
Moreton-on-Lug Camp 67–68

**Hertfordshire**
33 Dancer's Hill Camp 69
Arches 69
Batford Camp 68
Gorhambury Park 69
Hatfield Hyde 68
Ledbury Camp 68
Lemsford 68
Meesden 69
Royston Heath Camp 68
Stanborough 68
Wynches Camp 69

Hess, Rudolph 23, 35–36

Interrogation Centre 23–26

**Isle of Man, The**
Isle of Man Camp 158
RAF Jurby 158

**Jersey**
Fort Regent 157

Kamp, Franz 187

**Kent**
Brissenden Green Camp 71
Coed-Bel Camp 71
Mabledon Camp 71
Mereworth Castle 71
Ministry of Works Camp 71
Royal Engineers Bridging Camp 72
Shorncliffe Camp 70

Somerhill Camp 70
St Radigund's Camp 72
Summer House 71
Walderslade Camp 70
Woodchurch Camp 70

Kersting, Juergen 168
Kick, Leonhardt 177

**Kincardineshire**
North Hill Camp 137

**Kirkcudbrightshire**
St Andrew's Hall 137

Knochlein, Fritz 17–18
Kuehne, Armin 167–168

**Lancashire**
Bank Hall Camp 73
Brook Mill Camp 74
Camp A 74
Fort Crosby 74
Garswood Park 73
Glen Mill 72
Melland Camp 73
Newton Camp 73–74
Ormskirk 73
Penketh Hostel 74
Warth Mills 73

**Leicestershire**
Barkby Camp 76
Farndon Road Camp 75
Garendon Park 75
Gaulby Billesdon 75
Hathern Camp 76
Knighthorpe Camp 75
Old Dalby Camp 76
Old Liberal Club 75
Quorn Camp 75
Scraptoft 74
Shady Lane 76

**Lincolnshire**
Allington 76–77
Canwick Camp 79
Castlethorpe Camp 78
Donna Nook Airfield 79
Fulney Park 78
Heath Camp 78
Horbling Camp 77
Kirmington Camp 79
Moorby Camp 77
Nether Headon Camp 77
Pingley Farm Camp 77
Potterhanworth Booths 80
Rectory Camp, The 78
Stamford Camp 76
Usselby Camp 79
Weelsby Camp 78
Willingham House 78–79

**London**
22 Hyde Park Gardens 80
Becton Marshes Camp 81
Carpenter's Road Camp 81
Hampton Park 81
Newlands House 81
Scrubs Lane Camp 81
Shooters Hill 82

**Middlesex**
Capel House Camp 84
Cockfosters Camp 83
Ministry of Works Camp, The 83
Osterley Park Camp 84
Oxhey Lane Camp 83
Rayner's Lane 83
Trent Park Camp 82, 83
West Ridge Camp 84

**Midlothian**
Dalmahoy Camp 138
Deer Park Camp 139
Donaldson School 137–138
Duddingston Camp 139

Inchdrewer House 138
Mortonhall 139
Woodhouselee Camp 137

**Monmouthshire**
Claremont, Abergavenny 155
Llanmartin Camp 155
Llanover Park Camp 155–156
Mardy Camp 155
Mount Camp, The 155
New Inn Camp 156

**Montgomeryshire**
Glandulas Camp 156

Mount Kenya 173

**Norfolk**
Deopham Green 85–86
Hempton Green Camp 84
Kilverstone Hall 86
Kimberley Park 85
Mousehold Heath Camp 85
North Lynn Farm Camp 86
Snettisham Scalp 85
Sutton Bridge 85
Uplands Camp 85
Wolterton Camp 86

**Northamptonshire**
Boughton Park Camp 86–87
Byfield Camp 87
Hill Farm Estate 86
King's Cliffe 88
Park Farm 87
Weedon Camp 88

**Northumberland**
Byreness Camp 91
Darras Hill Camp 89–90
Featherstone Park Camp 88–89
Hetton House Camp 90
Kitty Brewster Farm 90
Lord Mayor's Camp 90

Tyne J Camp 91
Wooler Camp 90

**Nottinghamshire**
Boughton Camp 93–94
Carburton Camp 93
Carlton Hall 91
Norton Camp 92
RAF Camp Langar 93
Serlby Hall Camp 91
Tollerton Hall Camp 92
Wollaton Hall Park Camp 91–92

**Orkney Islands**
Lamb Holm 140–141
Rockworks Camp, The 141
Warebanks Camp 139–140

**Oxfordshire**
Eynsham Park 95
Graven Hill 95
Harcourt Hill Camp 94
Horgard Barracks 95
No 9 Tented Camp 95
North Camp 94
Old Windmills Camp 94
Shed D35 95
Shotover House 95

Pallme-Koenig, Erich 167

**Pembrokeshire**
Haverfordwest 156

Pentonville Prison 167

**Perthshire**
Balhary Camp 141–143
Calvine Camp 144
Cultybraggan Camp, Comrie 143–144
Cowden Camp 144
Errol Airfield 145
Methven Airfield (Loanleven) 145

Pluschow, Oberleutnant Gunther 159
Political Warfare Executive 177–178
Prisoner of War Interrogation Section 17–18
Propaganda Section 177

**Radnorshire**
Greenfield Farm 156
Pendre Camp 156

**Renfrewshire**
Patterton Camp 145

Rettig, Gerhardt 167–168
Rheinwiesenlager (Rhine Meadow Camps) 22–23

**Ross**
Brahan Castle 146

Rosterg, Sergeant Major Wolfgang 163–168
Roth, Peter 186–187

**Roxburghshire**
Sunlaws Camp 146

Rundstedt, Field Marshal von 23, 50l 153

Schaffer, Lagerfuehrer 171
Schmittendorf, Emil 167–168
Schnabel, Leutnant Heinz 162–163

**Shropshire**
83 Ordnance Supply Depot 98
Acksea Camp 96–97
Adderley Hall 97
Davenport House 97–98
Green Fields Camp 96
Hawkstone Park 97
Mile House 96

Prees Heath 96
Sheet Camp 97
Sheriffhales Camp 97
South Camp 98
St Martin's Camp 96
Wilcott Camp 98

**Somerset**
Ashton Court 98
Barwick House Camp 99
Brockley Camp 99
Colley Lane Camp 98
Cross Keys Camp 99–100
Goathurst Camp 99
Houndstone 100–101
Penleigh Camp 99
Stoberry Park Camp 100

**South Lanarkshire**
Douglas Castle 146
Happendon Camp 146
Moor Camp, The 146

**Staffordshire**
Flaxley Green Camp 101
Halfpenny Green Lawn Camp 102
Loxley Hall Camp 102
Pendeford Hall Camp 102
Shugborough Park Hospital 102
Stretton Hall Camp 103
Teddesley Hall Camp 103
Wolseley Road Camp 102

**Stirlingshire**
Abbey Craig Park 147
Castle Rankine Camp 146–147

**Suffolk**
Botesdale 103
Debach Airfield 104–105
Ellough Airfield 104
Flixton Airfield 104
Hardwick Heath Camp 104

Redgrave Park Hospital 104
Victoria Camp 103–104

Sulzbach, Herbert 88–89, 166–168

**Surrey**
Barnhouse Farm 106
Kempton Park Camp 105
Kingwood Camp 105
Merrow Down Camp 105
Old Dean Common Camp 106
Raynes Park Camp 106
Ruskin Avenue 105
Topsite 106
Westonacres Camp 106

**Sussex**
Brook House 107
Kingsfold Camp 107
No 2 Camp 108
Normanhurst Camp 107
Seafield School 107–108

**Sutherland**
Earl's Cross House 148

Thornan, Major Willi 165
Thornley, Lieutenant Colonel
  Ronald 176–180
Trautmann, Bert 41, 45–46, 186–186

Vaughan, Keith 112

Wallace Monument, The 147
Wappler, Oberleutenant Harry
  162–163

**Warwickshire**
Arbury Hall 109
Barby Camp 110
Birdingbury Camp 109
Castle Camp 108–109
Cloister Croft 108
Ettington Park Camp 108

Long Marston Camp 108
Marlborough Farm Camp 109–110
Merevale Hall Camp 109
Number 3 Camp 110
Racecourse Camp 109
Stoneleigh Camp 110
Stratford-upon-Avon Camp 109

Werra, Franz von 49–50, 159
Weschke, Karl 58
Wheatley, John 166–168

**Wigtownshire**
Culreoch Camp 149
Holm Park Camp 148
Sheuchan School 149
ST2 and Leffnoll 148–149

**Wiltshire**
Aliwal Barracks 113
Ashton Gifford Camp 112
Eastern Grey Camp 111
Eden Vale Camp 111
Hill Camp 112–113
Le Marchant Camp 111
Lopscombe Corner Camp 112
Military Hospital 111–112
Stratton Factory Camp 112

**Worcestershire**
Blackmore Camp 114–115
Fladbury golf course 114
Longbridge Camp 113
Perdiswell Hall 114
Recreation Ground Camp 113–114

**Yorkshire**
Bramham Number 1 Camp 116
Butcher Hill 121
Butterwick Camp 120
Centenary Road 122
Cowick Hall 122
Dog and Duck Cottage 121
Eden Camp 117, 118

Gilling Camp 116
High Hall Camp 119
Lodge Moor Camp 116
Military Hospital in Naburn 120
Norton Camp 121
Overdale Camp 117
Post Hill Camp 117
Potters Hill 119
Racecourse at Ripon 119
Racecourse Camp 116
RAF Burn airfield 122
Ravensfield Park Camp 121–122
Sandbeds Camp 117
Scriven Hall Camp 118

Searchlight Site Camp 122
Stable Road Camp 122
Stadium Camp 122
Station Road in Tadcaster 122
Storwood Camp 117
Thirkleby Camp 118
Thomas Street 122
Thorpe Hall 121
Urebank Camp 121
Welton House 119
Weston Lane Camp 120

Zuchlsdorff, Kurt 167
Zuncheddu, John Salvatore 188

*Military Airfields in Britain During the Second World War*
**by Jon and Diane Sutherland**

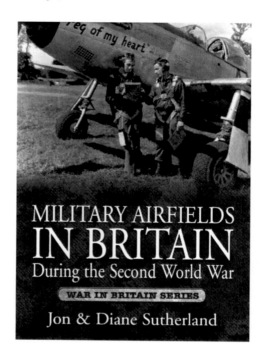

This book, the second in the War in Britain series, focuses on the British airfields which were used by the military in the Second World War. Military history experts, Jon & Diane Sutherland, investigate the locations of these airfields and why they were chosen, together with the physical and personal changes made to the surrounding areas, as well as the effects on the local community with the influx of strangers.

They reveal the legacy of the airfields and their specially created communities after the war. Did the buildings fulfil other uses in peacetime or were they and the runways just left to rot, a crumbling reminder of the losses of war?

**Available from all good booksellers and as an eBook for all eReaders**

ISBN 978-1-78095-017-4

*For more details and to see our other books, visit www.GoldenGuidesPress.com*

***Death and Destruction on the Thames in London***
**by Anthony Galvin**

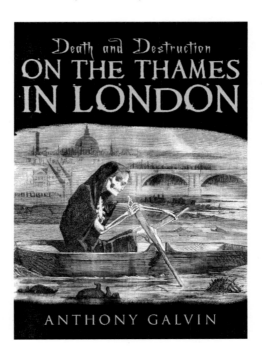

The first in the Death and Destruction series which will focus on different subjects or places. Starting with the Thames in London, this book explores the tragedies and enforced changes on and along the Thames, including fires (the Great Fire of London and Parliament burning down), ships sinking, wartime bombs and buildings destroyed, including York House on the Embankment whose archway shows the changing banks of the river thanks to Victorian intervention. It explores the tragic history of London's bridges, people dying during their creation, famous failed suicides and a strange case of assassination with an umbrella on Waterloo Bridge.

The tide of history along the Thames will be examined, including the infamous last journeys through Traitors' Gate. As well as the notable and bizarre deaths, the murders, suicides and executions, the book explores the positive life-saving methods in place, including the Thames Barrier.

**Available from all good booksellers and as an eBook for all eReaders**

ISBN 978-1-78095-007-5, £12.99

*For more details and to see our other books, visit www.GoldenGuidesPress.com*

## *The Classic Guide to Famous Assassinations*
### by Sarah Herman

Discover more about the famous assassinations in history throughout the world, from familial betrayal to power-lust and death by umbrella. A must-read guide to some of the most famous and most extraordinary assassinations committed – with a few conspiracy theories on the side.

Other books in the series include *The Classic Guide to King Arthur* by Dr Keith Souter.

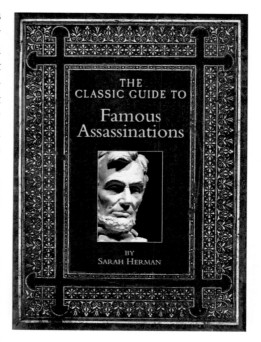

*Did you know:*

- President James Garfield died because his surgeons failed to wash their hands when fishing around in his body for bullets – after using a metal detector to try to find the bullets…
- Senator Huey Long died after doctor failed to notice his kidney had been perforated when he was shot. He died of internal bleeding two days later
- Bonaparte survived an assassination attempt when his snuff was replaced by poison
- Churches were popular places of assassination, with victims including St Peter of Arbues, Thomas à Becket, Alberta Williams King (Martin Luther King's mother) and Daniil Sysoyev

**Available from all good booksellers and as an eBook for all eReaders**

ISBN 978-1-78095-014-3, £9.99

*For more details and to see our other books, visit www.GoldenGuidesPress.com*

## The Classic Guide to King Arthur
### by Dr Keith Souter

The second in the Classic Guides series is full of fascinating facts about the main Arthurian legends, its characters and the symbolism of the legend throughout the ages, including a belief during the War that King Arthur would return to defend Britain in its hour of need.

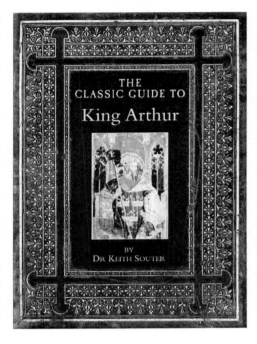

The chapter 'Who, What, Where and When in Arthur's Realm' explores different aspects of the legend, including the characters and locations from the tales – such as the castles and magical weapons from the stories. Dr Keith Souter also investigates the stories of King Arthur and his knights in literature, art, film and TV, and why we're still captivated by the centuries' old legend.

Other books in the series include *The Classic Guide to Famous Assassinations* by Sarah Herman.

### *Did you know....?*
- Sir Gawain's mighty steed was caused Gringalet
- Lancelot's main castle was called Castle Joyous Gard – believed to be either Alnwick or Bamborough Castles
- King Arthur's sword was famously called Excalibur – but did you know his spear was named Ron?

**Available from all good booksellers and as an eBook for all eReaders**

ISBN 978-1-78095-006-8, £9.99

*For more details and to see our other books, visit www.GoldenGuidesPress.com*

## *Sylvia Pankhurst: The Rebellious Suffragette*
## by Shirley Harrison

*'Her depiction of the lonely Sylvia... is an absorbing one'* The Independent on Sunday

*'Diligent biography of Sylvia'* Daily Mail

*'A riveting story'* The Lady

*'A skillfully balanced and very readable narrative'* The BookBag

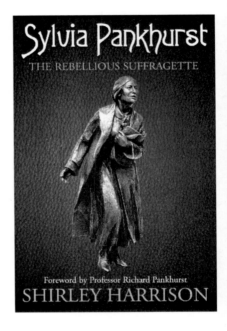

Shirley Harrison's acclaimed biography, with a foreword by Professor Richard Pankhurst, shows that Sylvia Pankhurst was more than a one-issue campaigner. She was thrown out of the Suffragettes by her mother, Emmeline, and sister, Christabel, when she refused to follow their more violent lead and insisted on helping women in the East End, forming an alternative group to the Suffragettes, and also helped men in need.

The most arrested Suffragette, Sylvia was Keir Hardie's lover, argued with Lenin, was on Hitler's arrest list and put under watch by Mussolini. She fought for better rights for Indians under British Rule and was given a state funeral in Ethiopia after helping them win independence against fascist Italy.

There is currently a campaign to erect a statue of Sylvia Pankhurst opposite the Houses of Parliament.

**Available from all good booksellers and as an eBook for all eReaders**

ISBN 978-1-78095-018-1, £17.99

*For more details and to see our other books, visit www.GoldenGuidesPress.com*